MPRE

STUDY GUIDE

2024-2025

- 📓 **Note-Taking Techniques:** Discover various methods for taking effective and organized notes during lectures or while reading textbooks.
- 💬 **Critical Thinking Skills:** Develop your ability to analyze, evaluate, and synthesize information to make informed decisions and solve problems.
- ⏰ **Time Blocking and the Pomodoro Technique:** Learn about time management techniques like time blocking and the Pomodoro Technique to enhance productivity
- 🧠 **Stress Relief Strategies:** Overcome exam anxiety with mindfulness, relaxation exercises, and mental resilience techniques.
- 📓 **Practice Makes Perfect:** Explore the importance of practice exams, sample questions, and mock tests, and understand how to analyze your performance to identify areas for improvement.
- ⚫ **Test-Taking Tactics:** Master the art of answering different types of questions, managing your time during the exam, and maintaining focus under pressure.

The following is a disclaimer of liability:

The goal of this book is to provide the reader with background information on the numerous topics that are discussed throughout the book. It is offered for sale with the understanding that neither the author nor the publisher are engaged in the practice of providing professional advice of any type, including but not limited to advice pertaining to legal matters, medical matters, or other matters. In the event that one need the aid of a professional, one must seek the assistance of an experienced professional who is qualified to provide it.

This book has been laboriously labored over in an effort to make it as accurate as is humanly feasible, and it has taken a lot of labor. However, there is a possibility that there are inaccuracies, both in the typography and the actual content of the article. The author and publisher of this book do not accept any responsibility or liability to any third party for any loss or damage caused, or represented to have been caused, directly or indirectly, by the information that is included in this book. This rule applies to any loss or harm that may have been caused, or is suspected of having been caused, by the information that is presented in this book.

This information is provided "as is," without any guarantees or warranties regarding its completeness, accuracy, usefulness, or timeliness. The information is presented "as is" without any guarantees or warranties of any kind. The reader is highly encouraged to seek the opinion of a certified expert or professionals in the field in order to obtain the most up-to-date knowledge that is currently available.

information and compiled data.

In no way, shape, or form does the viewpoints or policies of any specific organisation or professional body come over in this book in any kind whatsoever. Any slights that could be interpreted as being directed toward specific individuals or groups were not intended, despite the fact that they may have occurred.

TABLE OF CONTENT

STUDY GUIDE

Introduction

About the MPRE
The Importance of the MPRE
Preparing for Success

Chapter 1: Understanding the MPRE

What Is the MPRE?
Purpose and Significance of the MPRE
MPRE Format and Scoring
MPRE vs. Bar Exam

Chapter 2: Registration and Scheduling

Registration Process
Important Dates
Scheduling Tips
Accommodations for Special Needs

Chapter 3: Preparing for the MPRE

Creating a Study Plan
Recommended Study Materials
Self-Assessment
Study Groups
Balancing MPRE Prep with Law School

Chapter 4: The Model Rules of Professional Conduct

Overview of the Model Rules
Commonly Tested Rules
Learning Key Definitions
Case Examples
Model Rules by Subject Matter

Chapter 5: Scope of Representation and Allocation of Authority

Duty of Loyalty and Diligence
Conflicts of Interest
Authority and Responsibilities of a Lawyer

Chapter 6: Client-Lawyer Relationship

Formation of the Client-Lawyer Relationship
Communication with Clients
Fees and Trust Accounts
Safekeeping Property

Chapter 7: Regulation of Legal Profession

Admission and Discipline of Lawyers
Unauthorized Practice of Law
Responsibilities Regarding Non-Lawyer Assistants

Chapter 8: Conflicts of Interest

Types of Conflicts
Avoiding Conflicts
Imputed Disqualification
Consent and Waiver

Chapter 9: Competence and Legal Malpractice

Competence and Diligence
Legal Malpractice
Duty to Decline or Terminate Representation
Declining or Terminating Representation

Chapter 10: Confidentiality and Attorney-Client Privilege

The Duty of Confidentiality
Exceptions to Confidentiality
Attorney-Client Privilege
Work Product Doctrine

Chapter 11: Conflicts in the Legal Profession

Lawyer as Witness
Former Government Lawyer
Third-Party Neutrals
Permissible Restrictive Agreements

Chapter 12: Different Roles of the Lawyer

Advocacy and Negotiations
Third-Party Transactions
Nonprofit and Public Interest Organizations
Adjudicative Proceedings

Chapter 13: Judicial and Legal Officials

Maintaining Integrity and Impartiality
Ex Parte Communications
Law Reforms and Improvements
Reporting Professional Misconduct

Chapter 14: Regulation of Legal Services

Multijurisdictional Practice
The Sale of a Law Practice
Maintaining the Integrity of the Profession
Miscellaneous Ethical Considerations

Chapter 15: Taking Practice Exams

Simulated Practice Tests
Timing and Strategy
Reviewing and Learning from Mistakes
Building Confidence

Chapter 16: MPRE Test Day

Test Center Logistics
What to Bring
Strategies for Success
Staying Calm and Focused

Chapter 17: After the Exam

Waiting for Scores
Scoring and Grading
Next Steps
Preparing for the Bar Exam

Before we begin:

Congratulations for completing "MPRE Study Guide Secrets: Prep for the Multistate Professional Responsibility Examination 2024-2025." As you prepare to face the Multistate Professional Responsibility Examination (MPRE), we will delve into the complex world of legal ethics here in this all-encompassing handbook. This test is an important benchmark for both law students and practicing attorneys since it evaluates how well one understands the ethical principles and procedural procedures that govern the legal profession.

Interpreting statutes, negotiating settlements, and litigating cases in court are only a few of the many responsibilities that come with practicing law. It is a calling that requires an unrelenting dedication to upholding justice, as well as ethics and integrity as its foundational pillars. The public interest must always come first for lawyers, and they must do so while upholding the highest ethical and professional standards. This is a responsibility that is both singular and weighty.

Your understanding and ability to apply these ethical concepts, which are summarized in the Model Rules of Professional Conduct, will be evaluated based on your performance on the Model Professional Responsibility Examination (MPRE). These guidelines offer direction on how lawyers should conduct themselves, what responsibilities they owe to their clients and the legal system, and how they should traverse the intricate web of legal ethics. It is not enough to simply pass another test in order to be successful on the MPRE; rather, you must demonstrate that you are dedicated to these moral principles.

Why it's Important to Take the MPRE

Although the MPRE is not the same as the bar exam, passing it is still extremely important. In the majority of states and territories in the United States, passing the Multistate Professional Responsibility Exam is necessary to be admitted to the bar. Consequently, it is an important stepping stone on the path to becoming a registered attorney and should not be skipped. It is important not only because of the certificate, but also because it highlights how valuable it is to continue to earn the public's trust in the legal profession.

Infractions of the code of ethics that govern the legal profession can have severe repercussions, including disbarment, the destruction of a career, and even criminal prosecution. It is not merely a question of academic interest to comprehend and act in accordance with the ethical concepts that are evaluated on the MPRE; rather, it is a matter of maintaining one's professional status.

In this tutorial, we will provide you with the information and tactics you need to perform well on the MPRE. We will demystify the intricacies of the Model Rules, break down the fundamental ideas, and outline a step-by-step plan for you to follow on your way to becoming an expert. In addition, we will discuss the structure of the exam, the steps involved in registering for it, and efficient study methods to assist you in getting ready.

The Path to the MPRE Exam

The process of preparing for the MPRE starts well in advance of when you actually take the exam. It begins with the desire to pursue a career in law, a commitment to the legal profession, and a knowledge that ethical behavior is at the heart of what makes the legal profession tick. This path is an evolution, a process of transitioning from a law student or legal practitioner into an ethical guardian of justice. This trip is an evolution.

You will quickly understand that the Multistate Professional Responsibility Exam (MPRE) is more than just a test; rather, it is an embodiment of the goals and principles that guide the legal profession. It forces you to engage in critical reflection on a variety of ethical conundrums, just as you will be expected to do once you begin practicing law. The scenarios that you will experience during the MPRE are frequently subtle, and as a result, you will be required to traverse the delicate line that exists between right and wrong, as well as between your obligation to the client and your responsibility to the legal system.

You will find a guide that will assist you in navigating this adventure within the pages that follow. We will go over the fundamentals of the Model Rules of Professional Conduct, provide direction on the steps involved in the registration process, discuss effective methods for confronting the examination, and provide study plans and approaches.

Who Is Likely to Gain Advantages from Reading This Guide?

This handbook is intended to serve as a helpful reference for a wide variety of readers, including those who are:

Students of the Law: If you are in the process of studying law, regardless of whether it is your first or your final year, you will find this guide to be extremely helpful. Passing the Multistate Professional Responsibility Exam (MPRE) demonstrates that you are dedicated to upholding ethical standards in the legal profession.

Recent Law School Graduates: If you just finished law school and are getting ready to take the bar test, the Multistate Professional Responsibility Examination (MPRE) is an essential obstacle to overcome. You will be able to efficiently prepare with the help of our guide, which will save you significant time and ensure your success.

Legal Professionals: In order to keep your license active and protect your reputation, it is imperative for practicing attorneys to stay current with the ethical standards that govern their profession. This handbook provides an outstanding opportunity for you to update your knowledge and guarantee that you are in compliance with the most recent requirements.

Takers of the Bar Exam: When you are studying for the bar exam, it is imperative that you do not minimize the significance of the MPRE. If you are successful here, you will have an easier time getting admitted to the bar, and our guide will help you through the process.

The Things That Are to Be Expected

In the chapters that follow, we will conduct an in-depth investigation of the MPRE and break down its many different parts. In this section, we will discuss the Model Rules of Professional Conduct, which are considered to be the cornerstone of ethical legal practice.

You have the following to look forward to:

An in-depth look at the Model Rules of Professional Conduct, dissected into their component parts according to the topics they cover.

case studies taken from the real world to assist explain how these guidelines should be applied.

Methods for efficient preparation consisting of the development of a study plan, the establishment of study groups, and the performance of practice exams.

Helpful hints for time management on the day of the exam, as well as ways to maximize your score.

comprehensive explanations of sample questions taken from the practice test, designed to assist you in comprehending the various types of situations that may be presented to you.

In the appendix, for your convenience, you can find the complete text of the Model Rules.

Dedication, preparation, and an in-depth knowledge of legal ethics are all necessary ingredients for your success on the MPRE. This study guide is intended to equip you with the skills, information, and self-assurance necessary to perform exceptionally well on test day. Keep in mind that the process of getting there is just as essential as the final goal as you explore through its pages. Your dedication to the practice of law in an ethical manner demonstrates your dedication to the pursuit of justice, fairness, and the improvement of society.

Understanding the MPRE is covered in Chapter 1.

The Multistate Professional Responsibility Examination, also known as the MPRE, is an essential component of the legal profession and acts as a standard bearer for ethical practices within the industry. This chapter digs deeper into the meaning and relevance of the MPRE, elaborating on its structure, content, and the motivations that led to the creation of the exam.

What exactly is an MPRE?

The Multistate Professional Responsibility Examination, sometimes known as the MPRE for short, is a standardized, multiple-choice examination that evaluates applicants' knowledge and understanding of the standards of professional conduct that regulate the behavior of lawyers. The MPRE was developed by the National Association of Boards of Professional Responsibility Examiners. The National Conference of Bar Examiners (NCBE) is a non-profit organization that creates and administers standardized examinations for use in bar admissions. This examination is one of the standardized tests that the NCBE is responsible for.

The Multistate Professional Responsibility Examination (MPRE) is not the same as the Bar Examination, which evaluates a wider variety of legal knowledge and skills. Instead, the emphasis of the MPRE is solely placed upon the ethical duties and professional responsibilities that are incumbent upon lawyers. It is a specific test whose purpose is to guarantee that those seeking admission to the bar are not only well-versed in the law but also have a solid understanding of the ethical values that underpin the legal profession. This is done by ensuring that they can demonstrate an ability to recognize and avoid conflicts of interest.

The Importance of Having a Good MPRE Score

For a variety of reasons, the Multistate Professional Responsibility Examination (MPRE) is of the utmost importance in the legal profession:

A successful completion of the Multistate Professional Responsibility Exam (MPRE) is required for bar admission in the vast majority of jurisdictions in the United States. You will need to do well on the Multistate Professional Responsibility Examination (MPRE) if your goal is to become a licensed attorney.

Ethical Foundation: The Multistate Professional Responsibility Examination places a strong emphasis on the necessity of ethical behavior in the legal profession. The test guarantees that candidates have a thorough understanding of the ethical principles and laws that govern the conduct of lawyers, who play an essential part in the maintenance of the legal system.

Maintaining the confidence of the general public is an essential component of the legal profession. Customers place a high level of trust in their attorneys since they frequently have access to private and sensitive information. A candidate's success in the Multistate Professional Responsibility Examination (MPRE) is a validation of their dedication to ethical practice, which helps to create and preserve the public's faith in attorneys.

Preparation for Practice: The Multistate Professional Responsibility Exam (MPRE) is a very helpful preparation for the ethical difficulties that lawyers encounter throughout their professional lives. Candidates are encouraged to engage in critical thinking about difficult ethical conundrums and to apply the

Model Rules of Professional Conduct in real-world scenarios as a result of this.

Professional growth The Multistate Professional Responsibility Exam (MPRE) has the potential to be a useful instrument for the professional growth of practicing lawyers. It acts as a refresher on ethical norms, assisting them in remaining current with the ever-evolving concepts and rules.

The Format and Scoring of the MPRE

It is absolutely necessary for successful preparation to have an understanding of the structure and scoring of the MPRE. Let's look deeper into these different facets of the situation.

To format:

Multiple-Choice: Each question on the MPRE will have a number of different options to choose from. As of the most recent update, which I am aware of occurring in September 2021, there are a total of 60 scored questions and 10 unscored questions for the pretest. The results of the pretest questions are only kept for research purposes and will not be factored into your final grade. Because you won't be able to tell the difference between the questions on the scored test and the ones on the practice test, it's imperative that you take each question seriously.

Exam Sections: There are a total of 100 questions to be answered during the course of the examination, which is broken up into two distinct sessions, each lasting two hours and including 50 questions. In between the two sessions, there will be a 15-minute break for you to use. Because the answers to the questions in each session are intended to be provided in the time that is provided, effective time management is essential.

Your understanding of the Model regulations of Professional Conduct and other regulations relating to the professional conduct of attorneys will be tested using the questions in the Model Professional Responsibility Examination (MPRE). Your ability to recognize and address moral conundrums will be evaluated based on your responses to these questions.

Keeping score:

On the MPRE, your score is based on a scale that ranges from 50 to 150, and the passing score is often 75. This scaled score is derived from the raw score, which is the number of questions that are answered correctly by the participant. In order to maintain justice and continuity, the specific procedure for scaling may change from one administration to the next.

You should expect to receive your score for the MPRE roughly five weeks after the test. The MPRE is a criterion-referenced test, which means that your score is not based on how well other candidates perform; rather, it is based on an absolute standard. This is an important fact to keep in mind since it means that your score is not decided by how well other candidates perform.

Comparison between the MPRE and the Bar Exam

It is essential to make a distinction between the Multistate Professional Responsibility Examination (MPREE) and the Bar Examination since the two tests are designed for different objectives and cover different ground.

The rules of professional behavior and ethical standards in the legal profession are the exclusive focal point of the MPRE. It is a highly specialized test that evaluates a candidate's knowledge of ethical concepts as they relate to the practice of law. The Multistate Professional Responsibility Examination (MPRE) is required to be passed in order to obtain a license to practice law in the majority of states.

Exam for Admission to the Bar In contrast, the examination for admission to the bar is an all-encompassing examination that evaluates a candidate's knowledge of numerous subfields of law, such as constitutional law, contracts, torts, criminal law, and more. In addition to that, it consists of essay questions and a performance test. In order to become a licensed attorney, you are required to first pass the bar exam, which is a test that covers a considerably wider variety of topics related to legal knowledge and skills.

Registration and Appointment Scheduling are Discussed in Chapter 2.

The process of registering for and scheduling the Multistate Professional Responsibility Examination (MPRE) is the first step on the path to achieving a passing score on this examination. This chapter includes in-depth information about these important first steps, guiding you through the administrative requirements, deadlines, and techniques for a more streamlined experience.

The Process of Registration

Before delving into the finer points of the registration procedure, it is vital to have a firm grasp on the fact that the procedure itself may vary over the course of time, as well as the specific needs. For this reason, it is absolutely necessary to consult either the official website of the National Conference of Bar Examiners (NCBE) or the official website of the jurisdiction in which you intend to take the MPRE in order to obtain the most recent information. The following is a summary of the steps involved in the registration procedure, as of my most recent knowledge update in September 2021:

Eligibility Before you sign up for the MPRE, you need to make sure that you are eligible to take the exam according to the standards established by the NCBE and the jurisdiction in which you wish to practice. One of these requirements is often meeting the academic standards of a law school that has been accredited by the American Bar Association (ABA) or having graduated from such a school. Candidates who do not have a J.D. may also be eligible.

Create an Account with the NCBE In order to register for the MPRE, you will need to first create an account on the online platform that the NCBE provides. This account will act as the nerve center for all of your MPRE-related actions, from the moment you register to the moment you submit your scores.

Choose Your Exam Date and Location: The NCBE provides many opportunities to take the MPRE throughout the course of the year. You are free to choose the date and place of the examination that best accommodates your needs and interests. It is in your best interest to organize ahead of time because popular exam dates and locations may fill up rapidly.

Pay the Exam price: In order to finish registering for the exam, you are going to need to pay the exam price. The total cost of the registration may be different for each jurisdiction and depending on whether you submit your application on time or not. Be remember to check the NCBE website for the most up-to-date fee information.

Special Accommodations You are required to make a request for special accommodations throughout the registration process if you need them because of a disability or another condition that qualifies you for them. The NCBE has established concrete protocols for submitting requests for such accommodations and documenting their use.

Examine the Handbook The NCBE offers a comprehensive MPRE Information and Registration Handbook for candidates to go through. Because it contains crucial information concerning registration, the format of the test, and the policies, it is absolutely necessary to read through this manual in its entirety.

Confirmation and entry Ticket: Once you have successfully registered for the exam and paid the associated price, you will receive a confirmation and entry ticket, most commonly in the form of an email. This document provides essential information regarding the location of the test, the time at which you must report for it, and the materials that you are permitted to bring with you to the examination.

identity Documents Needed: On the day of the exam, you will need to bring valid identity documents with you to the testing center. The requirements for identification are normally specified in the entry ticket, and they may consist of a photo ID provided by the government in addition to your admission ticket.

Keep in mind that the dates for registering are very important. If you miss a deadline, you might have to pay additional costs, choose from a smaller pool of test centers, or even lose the ability to take the exam on the date of your choice.

Dates That Are Crucial

It is essential to have a thorough understanding of the significant dates and cutoff times in order to successfully register for the MPRE. In most years, the NCBE will administer the MPRE on a quarterly basis. Since the specific dates are subject to change from one year to the next, you should check the NCBE website in order to obtain the most up-to-date information. Nevertheless, the following is a summary in broad strokes of the administration dates and registration periods for the MPRE:

The March Graduate Management Admissions Test is typically given at the end of March. Typically, the registration period for the March MPRE begins in December of the year prior and continues through February of the following year.

The August administration of the MPRE is often planned to take place during the first or second week of August. Typically, registration for the August MPRE begins in April and continues through the month of June.

The November MPRE is an exam that is traditionally given in the middle to later part of November. The registration period for the November exam typically begins in July and continues through the month of September.

It is crucial to be aware that although late registration typically comes with an additional price, it is sometimes still possible to sign up for an event for a little amount of time after the usual registration deadline has passed. If you miss the deadline for late registration as well, it's possible that you'll have to wait until the following time the test is offered. As a result, you should make preparations well in advance and register for the exam as soon as you can if you want to ensure that you get the date and place of your choice.

Time Management Advice

A few critical considerations are necessary for the successful scheduling of your MPRE, including the following:

Make preparations in advance because the MPRE is not an easy test to pass. It is necessary to prepare, and the earlier you begin, the greater the likelihood that you will be successful. Find a day that works with the schedule you've set for your studies, and register for the event as early as possible.

How to Choose the Right Test Center When choosing a test center, it is important to take into consideration a number of variables, including its accessibility to your location, the modes of transportation it offers, and any personal preferences you may have. It is recommended that you make your decision and register as soon as possible in order to guarantee a position at one of the more popular testing locations.

Think About Your Study Schedule Keep in mind that the MPRE calls for specific amounts of time spent studying. When choosing a date for your exam, you should take into account your law school timetable, any work responsibilities, and any other obligations you have. You will want to make certain that you have sufficient time to get ready.

seek Accommodations in Advance If you need special accommodations because of a handicap or another condition that qualifies you for them, make sure to seek them as soon as possible during the registration process. Because it is possible that the process of seeking accommodations will take a lot of time, it is best to get started as soon as possible.

Examine the Admission Ticket As soon as you have your admission ticket, you should examine it very carefully to ensure that it is accurate. Verify the date, time, and place of the examination. On the day of the exam, double check that you have the proper identification as well as any items that are permitted.

Putting Yourself in the Shoes of the Exam It is useful to take practice examinations under timed conditions as the date of the actual exam draws nearer. This not only helps you organize your time more efficiently but also simulates the actual environment of the test.

Maintain Your Knowledge: Make sure to check your email and the website of the NCBE often for any announcements or updates concerning the MPRE. In order to have a trouble-free testing experience, it is vital to be informed about any modifications or new advancements.

The preparation for the MPRE is covered in Chapter 3.

Preparation is the most important factor in determining whether or not one will pass the Multistate Professional Responsibility Examination (MPRE). This section is devoted to assisting you in formulating a well-structured study plan, selecting appropriate study materials, and implementing tactics that will maximize the effectiveness of your educational experience. It is not enough to simply memorize information in order to pass the MPRE; you must also demonstrate an awareness of and ability to apply the ethical concepts that serve as the foundation of the legal profession.

Making a Study Schedule and Plan

Your success on the MPRE depends on having a comprehensive study plan that is properly planned. It assists you in effectively managing your time, ensuring that all relevant topics are covered, and constructing the necessary knowledge and abilities. The following is a step-by-step method that will assist you in developing an efficient study plan:

Assessing Your Knowledge: To begin, you should either take a diagnostic practice test for the MPRE or evaluate the curriculum you've completed on legal ethics. This preliminary evaluation will assist you in determining your areas of excellence and areas for improvement.

Establish Unambiguous Objectives: Outline both the target score you wish to reach and the time range in which you intend to do it. You may keep yourself motivated and on track by setting objectives that are SMART, which stands for precise, measurable, achievable, relevant, and time-bound.

Determining the total number of hours you have available for MPRE preparation is the first step in allocating time for study. Next, divide these total hours into daily or weekly study sessions as appropriate. Consider how much time you actually have available each day and act accordingly.

Acquire an Understanding of the Content: Get familiar with the Model Rules of Professional Conduct, which serve as the basis for the Model Professional Responsibility Ethic. The Model Rules address a wide range of issues pertaining to legal ethics, including client-attorney interactions, conflicts of interest, confidentiality, competency, and many others. Make a list of the essential ideas that you have to have a handle on.

Materials for Studying You should give careful consideration to the study materials you use (this topic will be covered in more detail later in the chapter). Make certain that you have access to credible study guides, practice questions, and any other reference materials that you might require.

Your time spent studying should be broken up into several pieces, with each day or week devoted to a particular category of material or set of guidelines. For instance, you could devote one week to the topic of conflicts of interest, and the week after that to the topic of secrecy.

Regular practice is essential; your study plan should include both actual and simulated tests, as well as practice questions. Your ability to apply what you've learned and do well on tests will improve as you engage in regular practice.

Track Your Performance: Make sure to keep a record of how well you did on both the tests and the practice questions. Determine the aspects of your performance that could use some work, and adapt your study strategy accordingly.

Review and Revision: At regular intervals, go back over the information you've learned to ensure that you fully comprehend it. As the date of the test draws closer, you should shift your attention to targeted review and practice examinations.

Take Timed Practice tests: In the weeks coming up to the MPRE, you should take timed practice tests in order to imitate the conditions of the actual test. On the day of the actual exam, this will assist you in managing your time more successfully.

Strive for a Healthy Balance Between Work, Life, and Studying: During the time that you are preparing for the MPRE, it is crucial to keep a balanced lifestyle. In order to avoid becoming burned out, you should make sure that you schedule in time for relaxation, physical activity, and social connections.

Do Not Hesitate to Seek Support: If there are particular subjects or ideas that are causing you difficulty, do not be afraid to seek support. This information might come from your lecturers, other students, or resources found online.

Materials Suggested for Academic Study

One of the most important aspects of your preparation for the MPRE is making sure you select the appropriate study resources. The following is a list of suggested references for your consideration:

Study Aids for the Official MPRE The National Conference of Bar Examiners (NCBE) provides study aids for the official MPRE. These study aids consist of practice questions and sample tests. Because they are so closely related to the actual test, these resources are extremely helpful.

Commercial Study Guides Several different publishers make available for purchase commercial study guides that have been developed expressly for the MPRE. These manuals often give a detailed introduction to the Model Rules of Professional Conduct, as well as practice questions, explanations, and an overall summary.

Model Rules of Professional Conduct: The actual Model Rules themselves are an invaluable resource. You may access them for free online and they serve as a model for other professionals to follow. It is imperative that you carefully read and comprehend each of the rules.

Materials from Your Law School Courses If you've ever taken a class on professional responsibility or legal ethics, the textbooks and lecture notes you used in that class can be extremely helpful resources to look back on.

Practice Tests Available Online There are a number of websites and preparation firms that offer online practice tests and questions that are designed to imitate the MPRE. Check to see that the providers of these resources have a good reputation.

Participating in or establishing an MPRE study group on your own can prove to be advantageous. Your ability to learn and remember content can be improved by having in-depth conversations with your classmates about key concepts and by working through sample questions together.

Evaluation by Oneself

Self-evaluation on a consistent basis is an essential component of successful MPRE test preparation. It enables you to evaluate your progress, recognize areas in which you may need some work, and modify your study plan in response to these findings. Consider the following strategies for your own personal evaluation:

Questions to Practice Always put in the time to practice questions in the format of the MPRE, both scored and unscored. Carefully go over your explanations and replies to the questions. Pay close attention to the questions that you responded incorrectly to or about which you had questions.

Exams That Are Exactly Like the Real Ones You should imitate the conditions of the real exam by taking full-length, timed practice exams. In order to evaluate your ability to manage your time effectively, you should strive to finish these assessments without being interrupted.

Maintaining a Record of Your Performance It is important to keep a record of how well you perform on both practice questions and actual tests. Take note of the subjects or ideas that present you with a regular difficulty. This will direct your efforts toward a more concentrated study.

analyze and Analysis: Once you have finished an exercise test, you should carefully analyze all of your answers. Learn from your mistakes by analyzing why you got certain questions wrong and understanding why you got certain questions wrong.

Modify your study schedule in accordance with the results of your self-evaluation, and adapt as necessary. Devote more of your time to the areas in which you need improvement, and continue to build on your successes.

Performance Metrics: Keep track of your grades on mock tests so that you may see how much you've improved over time. In an ideal world, you should notice an improvement in your performance as your comprehension of the content grows deeper.

Discussion Groups

Increasing your level of preparation by participating in or forming your own MPRE study group can be an efficient approach to do it. The following are some of the advantages of participating in a study group:

Learning Through Collaboration: Investigating difficult ethical situations and guidelines as a group can lead to improved levels of comprehension. Engaging in discourse on themes with one's contemporaries might yield a variety of opinions.

Participating in conversations: Participating in conversations provides you with the opportunity to practice articulating your thoughts and reasoning, which is beneficial for the written response questions on the MPRE.

Accountability Study groups are a helpful tool for maintaining accountability to one's own study routine. Knowing that the opinions of others are dependent on yours might serve as a source of motivation to maintain your dedication.

Sharing of Resources Members of a study group will frequently share resources with one another. These can include study questions, study guides, or helpful web information.

Emotional support is necessary because studying for a significant exam may be an extremely stressful experience. The feeling of loneliness that some exam takers may have can be alleviated by the provision of emotional support and encouragement that study groups offer.

When taking part in a study group, it is essential to lay out the group's objectives, the calendar for gatherings, and the expectations for members. Ensure that your group continues to foster an atmosphere that is productive and focused.

Finding a Healthy Balance Between Law School and MPRE Prep

The demands of schoolwork and other duties coexist for many law students while they prepare for the Multistate Professional Responsibility Examination (MPRE). It may be difficult to prepare for the MPRE while also meeting the requirements of your regular law school obligations, but this challenge is not insurmountable with good time management and self-discipline. The following are some techniques that can assist you in preserving this equilibrium:

Make a Timetable for Your Studies: Create a study schedule that is unmistakable, well-organized, and that includes specific blocks of time devoted to MPRE preparation. To avoid exhaustion and prevent burnout, schedule regular breaks.

Make the Most of the Resources Available at Your Law School It is important to make the most of the resources available at your law school, such as your law library, reference materials, and teachers. They are able to offer insightful advice and dependable help.

Maintain your efficiency by avoiding activities and distractions that will waste your time. Maintaining focus when you study and eliminating distractions will allow you to get the most out of your time.

Incorporate the MPRE into Courses If the law school you plan to attend provides a course on professional responsibility or ethics, you should think about enrolling in it at the same time as you prepare for the MPRE. The material from the course can be used to supplement your study.

Seek Flexibility: If it is at all possible, try to get some degree of flexibility in your law school schedule in order to meet the requirements of your MPRE preparation. Talk to your teachers and the academic counselors assigned to you about the predicament you're in.

Determine what your most important academic goals are and prioritize those. Even while the MPRE is significant, you shouldn't let it distract you from concentrating on how well you are doing in your legal studies.

Develop your ability to effectively manage your time so that you can study for the MPRE while also meeting the standards set forth by your law school. Calendars and to-do lists, among other organizational aids, can be of great use.

Maintain your health by paying attention to both your emotional and physical well-being. To keep one's mind clear and one's productivity high, it is necessary to engage in regular physical activity, to consume nutritious food, and to get a enough amount of sleep.

The Model Rules of Professional Conduct can be found in Chapter 4.

The Multistate Professional Responsibility Examination (MPRE) and, more generally speaking, ethical practice in the legal profession are both based on the Model Rules of Professional Conduct. In this chapter, we delve into these rules, analyzing their relevance as well as the common threads that run throughout them and the significant provisions that they contain. To do well on the Model Rule Examination (MPRE) and to develop into an ethical and responsible lawyer, it is absolutely necessary to comprehend the Model Rules.

An Introduction to the Model Rules

The Model guidelines of Professional Conduct, more commonly known to simply as the Model Rules, are a set of ethical guidelines that are intended to direct the behavior of attorneys practicing in the United States. They were developed as a model code for professional conduct by the American Bar Association (ABA), which is responsible for their creation. The Model Rules have had a significant impact on the development of ethical norms within the legal profession, and they are widely embraced by a variety of jurisdictions across the United States.

The Model Rules have the following key purposes in mind:

Clients' Rights and Property are Protected The standards provide a framework for attorneys to protect their clients' rights and property while acting in the best interests of their clients.

Protect the Honesty of the Legal System The Model Rules are designed to make certain that attorneys continue to protect the honor of the legal system by adhering to rigorous ethical standards and the primacy of the rule of law.

Keeping the public's trust in the legal system requires that attorneys always act in a manner that is consistent with the highest ethical standards. The Model Rules contribute to the maintenance of this trust.

Enhance the Reputation of the Profession The Model Rules are designed to improve the reputation of the legal profession by promoting professionalism, accountability, and responsibility among attorneys.

The Model Rules are comprised of a variety of rules, comments, and guidance notes that address a broad spectrum of potential ethical dilemmas that lawyers may face in the course of their professional careers. These guidelines assist attorneys in resolving difficult ethical conundrums that arise in the practice of law and ensure that their behavior is congruent with the guiding principles of the legal profession.

The Model Rules Share a Few Common Themes

Despite the fact that the Model Rules include a wide variety of ethical principles, there are a few recurring themes that can be found across the rules:

Duty Owed to the Client A number of standards place an emphasis on the fundamental obligation of a lawyer toward their clients. A lawyer's ethical obligations include looking out for their client's best interests, diligently advocating on their behalf, and protecting their client's privacy.

Concerning the Avoidance of Conflicts of Interest The Model Rules address the problem of conflicts of interest in a variety of settings. It is imperative for lawyers to steer clear of scenarios in which their own personal interests may compete with those of their clients. The rules offer direction on how to address and resolve disagreements in the event that they materialize.

Maintaining Competence: Clients have the right to demand competent legal assistance from their attorneys. This necessitates ongoing education, the development of skills, and the maintenance of a current awareness of legal developments.

Sincerity and truthfulness: In the practice of law, sincerity and truthfulness are two of the most important principles. It is expected of lawyers to tell the truth in all of their conversations, including those with the courts, their clients, and any other parties involved.

Protecting the Confidentiality of Client Information Lawyers have a professional responsibility to maintain client confidentiality. This obligation goes beyond the attorney-client confidentiality and is essential for maintaining faith in the legal system.

connections in the Profession The Model Rules cover the professional connections that exist between lawyers and their clients, as well as between opposing parties and the court. Respect in professional relationships can be fostered with the help of these guidelines for interactions.

Independence in the Practice of Law: Clients of lawyers should expect them to use their own independent professional judgment when representing them. They have to steer clear of any conflicts or inappropriate influences that could cloud their judgment.

The Model Rules respect lawyers' positions as officers of the court and highlight their responsibility to protect the integrity of the legal system and serve the public interest. This is because the Model Rules recognize lawyers' duties as officers of the court.

The Model Rules' Most Important Provisions

It is vital, in order to get a full grasp of the Model Rules, to investigate significant provisions across different sections of the document. While we won't be able to go over every rule in great depth here, we will concentrate on some of the most relevant provisions:

Rule 1.1: Competence states that a lawyer is required to provide a client with competent representation. To provide competent representation, one must have the legal knowledge, expertise, level of detail, and level of preparation that are reasonably required for the representation.

In order to properly represent their clients, lawyers need to have the information and abilities essential in the legal field.

It is necessary to engage in ongoing legal education in order to keep one's competence.

Preparing thoroughly for cases is an essential part of being competent.

Regulation 1.3: Diligence: "A lawyer shall act with reasonable diligence and promptness in representing a client."

On behalf of their clients, attorneys are expected to work expeditiously and diligently.

Because of this law, it is especially important to have legal representation that is both prompt and thorough.

Rule 1.4: Communication: According to "A lawyer shall keep the client reasonably informed about the status of the matter and promptly comply with reasonable requests for information."

It is expected of attorneys to maintain clear and productive communication with their clients at all times.

Customers have the right to be kept up to date with the development of their cases and to have their questions answered in a timely manner.

Rule 1.6: Protection of Confidentiality of Information "A lawyer shall not reveal information relating to the representation of a client unless the client gives informed consent, the disclosure is impliedly authorized to carry out the representation, or the disclosure is permitted by other rules."

This rule emphasizes the necessity of safeguarding the confidentiality of client information and the attorney-client privilege that exists between lawyers and their clients.

The guidelines only allow for a few number of exceptions to the rule of confidentiality, and each one needs to be justified.

Rule 1.7 of the General Rules Concerning Conflicts of Interest If the representation of the client would imply a concurrent conflict of interest, a lawyer is not allowed to represent the client. If the representation of one client will be directly adverse to the interests of another client, then there is a concurrent conflict of interest. If there is a significant risk that the representation of one or more clients will be materially limited by the lawyer's responsibilities to another client, a former client, or a third person, or by the lawyer's own personal interest, then there is also a concurrent conflict of interest.

Conflicts of interest, whether they are direct or have a major potential for limitation, must be avoided at all costs by lawyers.

If there is a conflict that has to be managed, the regulation demands that informed permission be obtained from all of the impacted customers.

Rule 1.15, which is titled "Safekeeping Property," states that a lawyer must maintain the property of clients or third parties that is in their custody in connection with a representation distinct from the practitioner's own property. The funds are required to be stored in a separate account, which must be managed in the state in which the attorney's office is located.

Attorneys have the duty to handle client funds and those belonging to third parties in an appropriate manner and to keep them distinct from their own property at all times.

Keeping accurate records is absolutely necessary for maintaining transparency.

8.4: Misconduct: According to "It is professional misconduct for a lawyer to: (a) violate or attempt to violate the Rules of Professional Conduct, knowingly assist or induce another to do so, or do so through the acts of another; (b) commit a criminal act that reflects adversely on the lawyer's honesty, trustworthiness, or fitness as a lawyer in other respects; (c) engage in conduct involving dishonesty, fraud, deceit, or misrepresentation; (d) engage in conduct that is prejudicial to the administration of justice."

This rule addresses professional misconduct, which includes violations of the Model Rules as well as criminal activities, dishonesty, and behavior that compromises the integrity of the legal system.

The Process of Getting Ready for Some Rule-Based Model Questions

On the Model Procedures and Procedures Enforcement Exam (MPRE), you will be asked questions that test both your knowledge of the Model Rules and your ability to apply that knowledge. Take into consideration the following tactics in order to successfully prepare:

Read the Rules, and Make Sure You Comprehend Them First, Make Sure You Read and Comprehend the Model Rules. It is absolutely necessary to have a solid understanding of the regulations themselves.

Pay Attention to the Important Provisions: Pay careful attention to the essential provisions that were discussed before, as they are the cornerstone of conducting ethical legal practice.

Questions to Practice: In this section, you will work through practice questions modeled after the MPRE that evaluate your ability to apply the rules to real-world settings. You can locate these questions in the official MPRE study materials, as well as in preparation courses and internet sites.

Analyze Hypothetical Situations As a practice activity, you should analyze hypothetical scenarios and determine whether or not they entail ethical violations or conflicts based on the Model Rules.

Please go to the Official Commentary: The comments and notes of explanation that accompany the Model Rules offer illuminating and helpful perspectives on how the rules should be interpreted. They can be especially helpful in guiding your understanding of the complexities inherent in various ethical scenarios.

In the event that you find yourself in a difficult situation or are uncertain about a particular regulation, you should seek clarification by speaking with your professors, mentors, or peers. The discussion of different ethical issues can lead to a greater level of comprehension.

Exam Simulations: Incorporate timed, full-length mock tests into your study routine as part of your preparation. You will grow more used to the structure of the MPRE as well as the time limits through the use of this.

Scope of representation and allocation of authority are the topics covered in Chapter 5.

Lawyers can use the Model Rules of Professional Conduct as a guide to determine the extent of their client relationships and how authority should be distributed among themselves and their clients. This chapter dives into the ethical principles and standards that govern certain facets of legal practice and provides an in-depth examination of those topics. It is necessary for ethical, effective, and responsible legal representation to have a solid understanding of the boundaries and duties that come along with lawyer-client relationships.

Defining the Boundaries of the Area Represented

A lawyer's position in a given case can be defined in terms of its breadth and confines by referring to the "scope of representation." It is vital for attorneys to explicitly identify the bounds of their interaction with their clients. This allows the attorneys to better manage their clients' expectations and prevents any misconceptions from occurring. This idea is discussed in Model Rule 1.2, which is as follows:

Rule 1.2: The Boundaries of the Representation and Who Has the Authority to Act

"(a) A lawyer is obligated to abide by a client's decisions concerning the objectives of the representation and, as required by Rule 1.4, is required to consult with the client as to the means by which they are to be pursued. Paragraphs (c) and (d) of this rule apply only to the exceptions to this rule.

Any action that is impliedly permitted for the lawyer to do on behalf of the client in order to carry out the representation can be taken by the lawyer. The decision of a client's attorney regarding whether or not to settle a case must be respected. In a criminal proceeding, the client's attorney is required to respect the client's decision on the type of plea that will be entered, whether or not the client will renounce their right to a jury trial, and whether or not the client will testify.

"(b) A lawyer's representation of a client, including representation by appointment, does not constitute an endorsement of the client's political, economic, social, or moral views or activities."

"(c) A lawyer may limit the scope of the representation if the limitation is reasonable under the circumstances and the client gives informed consent."

"(d) A lawyer shall not counsel a client to engage, or assist a client, in conduct that the lawyer knows is criminal or fraudulent, but a lawyer may discuss the legal consequences of any proposed course of conduct with a client and may counsel or assist a client to make a good faith effort to determine the validity, scope, meaning, or application of the law."

Rule 1.2's Most Important Components

Objectives of the Client An attorney has an ethical obligation to respect the choices made by the client in reference to the goals of the representation. This includes making decisions regarding the path that will be taken to achieve those goals.

The ways by which the objectives will be achieved are a topic that must be discussed between the client and the attorney throughout the consultation process. Because of this conversation, clients are given the opportunity to provide input regarding the strategies and methods used in their representation.

Regarding the question of whether or not to reach a settlement, attorneys are required to respect the decisions made by their clients. In this matter, the decision ultimately rests with the customer.

Cases Involving Criminal Activity In cases involving criminal activity, attorneys are required to respect the decisions made by their clients regarding significant issues such as the acceptance of plea deals, the use of juries in trials, and whether or not the defendant would testify.

Endorsement and Limitation: The fact that a client is represented by an attorney does not in any way indicate that the attorney supports the client's choices on matters of belief or behavior. Under certain conditions and with the client's informed consent, attorneys are permitted to restrict the scope of the representation they provide.

Conducting Criminal or Fraudulent Activity It is unethical for attorneys to advise their clients to participate in criminal or fraudulent activity. However, they are able to explore the legal repercussions of potential actions with clients and help customers better grasp the law.

When it comes to understanding and following Rule 1.2, attorneys are required to strike a balance between respecting the autonomy of their clients and delivering legal representation that is efficient, ethical, and responsible. Clients have the right to make informed decisions regarding their legal affairs, and attorneys are obligated to respect those decisions as long as they are made in accordance with the law and ethical standards.

Relationships between Clients and Lawyers Regarding the Assignment of Authority

In the relationship between a lawyer and a client, the proper distribution of power is an essential component of ethical practice. It establishes which decisions are the responsibility of the client and which belong to the lawyer. Rule 1.2 emphasizes the significance of the client's role in decision-making, but it also recognizes that the attorney has some of the responsibility for the outcome of the case. These divisions of power are important for ensuring that the attorney-client relationship is one that is both effective and ethical.

1. Determinations that fall under the client's purview:

The client has the ultimate authority to define the goals of the representation, thus it is in their best interest to communicate those goals clearly. This includes establishing the aims of the legal matter as well as the outcomes that are intended. The client determines the goals, and the attorney is obligated to respect and adhere to those goals.

The clients are also in control of the means by which their goals are achieved, giving them full influence over this aspect of the process. Clients are ultimately responsible for determining the strategies, methods, and actions that are utilized in their legal affairs, with the assistance of their attorneys. While attorneys are required to confer with their clients and offer legal advice, the client is ultimately responsible for making the decision.

Decisions Regarding the Settlement Clients have the authority to decide whether or not a legal dispute will be settled. It is possible for attorneys to advise clients on the positives and negatives of reaching a settlement, but ultimately, the choice is with the client. When it comes to making settlement decisions, attorneys should never use coercion or undue influence on their clients.

Decisions Regarding Criminal matters When it comes to criminal matters, the client has the authority to make crucial decisions, such as whether or not to accept a plea bargain, whether or not to forgo their right to a jury trial, and whether or not the client would testify. Although customers are required to receive pertinent information and counsel from their attorneys, the decisions made by clients are legally binding.

2. Determinations that are under the Attorney's purview:

Professional Judgment Lawyers are entrusted with the responsibility of using their professional judgment when it comes to the formulation of both tactical and strategic plans. This includes deciding which legal arguments to pursue, the order in which legal actions will be taken, and the manner in which evidence will be presented in court.

The scope of legal representation may be limited by a client's attorney, but the restriction must be reasonable given the specifics of the case, and the client's permission must be obtained after receiving adequate information. The treatment of only some aspects of a case or the decision not to pursue particular legal routes are both examples of such restrictions.

Lawyers have an ethical responsibility to ensure that their acts and judgments are in line with the rules and duties that govern the profession. During the entirety of the representation, they are obligated to conduct themselves in a manner that is ethical, honest, and with integrity.

Legal Consequences: Attorneys have the ability to discuss with their clients the potential legal repercussions of various courses of action. This requires maintaining the client's right to make their own decisions while simultaneously educating them on the possible legal consequences of their actions.

Conduct That Is Known to Be Illegal or Fraudulent Attorneys are not allowed to advise their clients to take part in behavior that the attorney is aware of being illegal or fraudulent. However, they are free to analyze the repercussions and implications of such activities from a legal standpoint.

Finding a Happy Medium Between Client Independence and Attorney Knowledge

In the context of attorney-client relationships, the delegation of authority serves to strike a balance between the competing values of client autonomy and attorney expertise. It recognizes the client's right to have the last say in decisions that influence their legal matters while simultaneously recognizing the professional judgment and ethical duties of the attorney.

Respect for the Client's Autonomy The Model Rules place a significant focus on protecting and honoring the client's right to their own autonomy. The client always has the right to make decisions regarding the legal goals, strategies, and settlements pertaining to their case. This independence is absolutely necessary for the attorney-client relationship to function well.

Legal Knowledge, Experience, and Expertise Lawyers bring to the table their legal knowledge, experience, and expertise. Clients receive guidance and advise from them as they navigate difficult legal issues thanks to the services they offer. Attorneys are required to use their professional judgment and come up with strategic judgments while keeping their clients' best interests in mind at all times.

Making Informed Decisions Obtaining clients' informed consent and maintaining open lines of communication are two of the most important factors in ensuring that clients make decisions with a complete comprehension of the repercussions those actions may have legally. It is the responsibility of attorneys to inform their clients about the potential drawbacks and advantages of the various legal options.

Ethical restrictions Lawyers are prohibited from advising their clients to participate in illegal or fraudulent behavior because they are subject to ethical restrictions that preclude them from doing so. This makes certain that legal representation continues to operate within the confines of the law and adheres to the standards of ethics.

Considerations of a Pragmatic Nature Regarding the Assignment of Authority

In order to successfully navigate the distribution of authority in lawyer-client relationships, one needs to have a sophisticated awareness of the client's needs, the current legal problem at hand, and ethical commitments. The following are some considerations to keep in mind:

Consultation: Lawyers should engage in meaningful consultations with their clients in order to investigate their goals as well as the methods that will be used to achieve those goals. For a relationship between an attorney and client to be fruitful, effective communication is essential.

Client Education Lawyers have a significant responsibility to educate their clients about the legal process, the range of possible outcomes, and the legal repercussions that can result from a variety of activities. Consent based on clients' level of understanding is required for decision making.

Judgement in the Profession Lawyers are expected to use their professional judgment when representing their clients and deciding on strategies that are in their clients' best interests. This includes making strategic choices in relation to legal arguments and legal proceedings.

Achieving a Balance in Autonomy It is vital to achieve a balance between the autonomy of the client and the skill of the lawyer. When providing ethical and competent legal representation, attorneys have a duty to respect their clients' right to make decisions about their cases.

Maintaining Integrity It is of the utmost importance to uphold ethical standards as well as the rule of law. It is unethical for attorneys to advise or aid clients in engaging in illegal or fraudulent behavior, and they have a professional obligation to uphold the highest standards of integrity in their practices.

Documentation: It is highly recommended that lawyers keep detailed records of all significant decisions, consultations, and client permission. This paperwork has the potential to serve as a record of the authority that was delegated as well as the informed consent that was given.

Communication Should Be Maintained: It is imperative that attorneys keep open lines of communication with their clients throughout the entirety of the legal engagement. This includes addressing any issues or queries that the client may have, as well as discussing developments, future changes in strategy, and other topics.

Relationship Between Client and Attorney (Chapter 6)

The most important aspect of the legal profession is the relationship that develops between a client and their attorney. In this chapter, we discuss the Model Rules of Professional Conduct, more notably Rules 1.4, 1.5, 1.6, 1.7, and 1.8, which address various facets of the interaction between a client and their attorney. For the sake of trust, communication, and the ethical standards that are the foundation of a successful legal practice, it is imperative that these guidelines be understood and adhered to at all times.

Communication is required under Rule 1.4.

It is absolutely necessary for attorneys and their clients to be able to communicate well with one another in order for the attorney-client relationship to be effective. Rule 1.4 of the Model Rules of Professional Conduct lays out the responsibilities that lawyers have with relation to contact with their clients as follows:

"(a) A lawyer is required to keep the client informed about the state of the case to the best of their ability.

(b) A lawyer is required to respond quickly and appropriately to reasonable requests for information.

(c) A lawyer has an obligation to clarify a matter to the extent that is reasonably necessary to enable the client to make informed decisions regarding the representation."

Principal Components of Rule 1.4:

Information That Is Reasonable Attorneys have a responsibility to keep their clients informed on the state of their legal cases to the best of their abilities. This involves delivering up-to-date information about the representation's progress, developments, and noteworthy events that have occurred.

Prompt Responses: Clients have the right to make reasonable information requests, and attorneys are obligated to respond to those requests as quickly as possible. This guarantees that customers have access to the data they require in order to make decisions based on accurate information.

Concerning the Explanation of topics Lawyers are obligated to explain legal topics to their clients to the extent that is reasonably necessary for the clients to make informed decisions concerning their representation. For this purpose, it may be necessary to provide clarification on legal ideas, procedures, or possible results.

comprehension of the Client It is important for attorneys to take into account the level of comprehension of their clients and alter their communication styles accordingly. It is crucial to ensure that customers can understand the information that is supplied to them.

Language and Clarity Lawyers are expected to communicate in a way that is straightforward and easy to comprehend. Explaining difficult concepts and legal jargon to clients in language that is easy to understand is essential to ensuring their satisfaction.

A client's ability to actively participate in their legal proceedings is increased when there is clear and open communication between the attorney and the client, which creates trust and encourages openness. It is essential to the connection between the client and the attorney, as it ensures that the client is kept informed and actively involved throughout the engagement.

Fees and Rules 1.5

In the relationship between an attorney and client, having fee agreements that are both transparent and ethical is essential. Rule 1.5 of the Model Rules discusses the obligations that are associated with fees and describes them as follows:

"(a) A lawyer shall not form an agreement for, charge, or collect an unreasonable fee or an unreasonable amount for expenses. A lawyer also shall not collect an unreasonable amount for expenditures. The following considerations are to be considered in order to determine whether or not a fee is reasonable:

(1) the amount of time and work that is required, as well as the uniqueness and difficulty of the questions that are involved, as well as the level of ability that is necessary to successfully perform the legal service;

(2) the possibility, if it is obvious to the client, that the attorney's acceptance of the particular work will prevent him or her from accepting other employment;

(3) the fee that is normally charged in the region for legal services that are analogous to those being provided;

(4) the quantity of money that was involved as well as the results that were obtained;

(5) any time constraints imposed by either the client or the situation;

(6) the type of professional relationship that is maintained with the customer and how long it has been maintained;

(7) the expertise, track record, and reputation of the lawyer or lawyers who will be providing the services; and

(8) if the fee is set in stone or based on performance."

Principal Components of Rule 1.5:

Fees That Are Reasonable It is against the law for lawyers to enter into contracts for, charge, or collect fees or other expenses that are not reasonable. Considerations such as the difficulty of the legal job, the outcomes that were reached, and the average prices charged in the area are among the aspects that go into determining whether or not a fee is acceptable.

Considerations for Determining Reasonableness The regulation includes a rundown of the considerations that both attorneys and clients need to make in order to determine whether or not a fee is acceptable. These considerations contribute to the establishment of a reasonable and equitable fee for legal services.

Transparency is something that should be maintained in the fee agreements of legal professionals. The client has the right to fully comprehend the rationale behind the fees and expenses that are being charged.

Contingent Fees: Contingent fees, in which the lawyer's income is contingent on the outcome of the case, are legal but are subject to ethical requirements. In this type of fee arrangement, the client is ultimately responsible for paying the attorney. The contingent fee arrangement must be fair and adequately disclosed, both of which are responsibilities of the attorney.

Communication: It is crucial to have clear and effective communication about the fees and charges. It is best practice for attorneys to sit down with their clients, discuss and agree upon fee arrangements, and take into account the ability of the client to pay.

Rule 1.5 has the purpose of ensuring that fee arrangements are equitable, open to public scrutiny, and based on a realistic evaluation of the legal services that are rendered. It encourages attorneys to examine a variety of variables when setting fees and to have honest conversations about remuneration with their clients.

Rule 1.6: All Information Must Be Kept Confidential

Rule 1.6 of the Model Rules emphasizes the significance of protecting the privacy of a client's information and underscores the foundational role that confidentiality plays in the attorney-client relationship:

"(a) A lawyer shall not reveal information relating to the representation of a client unless the client gives informed consent, the disclosure is impliedly authorized to carry out the representation, or the disclosure is permitted by paragraph (b) or required by paragraph (c)."

Principal Components of Rule 1.6:

Legal professionals have a responsibility to their clients to maintain the confidentiality of any information that relates to the representation of a client. This comprises information gathered during the representation, talks held about the client's case, and documents relevant to the client's legal matter.

There are several circumstances in which the obligation of secrecy does not have to be strictly adhered to, such as when the client offers informed consent to divulge information, when disclosure is impliedly approved in order to properly represent the client, or when disclosure is mandated by law. However, these circumstances are extremely rare.

Disclosures That Are Allowed Lawyers are allowed to reveal information to the degree that it is necessary to avoid a death or substantial bodily harm that is reasonably certain to occur, or to prevent a client from committing a crime or fraud that is substantially certain to result in substantial financial harm. These disclosures fall under the category of "permitted disclosures."

Trust Between Lawyers and Their Clients It is essential for trust to be kept between lawyers and their clients that client information be kept confidential. When communicating with their attorneys, clients really need to have the assurance that their information is safe.

Rule 1.6 expresses the ethical responsibility that lawyers have to safeguard the information of their clients and make certain that it is not released without the proper authorization or otherwise required by law. This principle is the bedrock upon which the attorney-client privilege and the sacredness of confidential attorney-client conversations are built.

Rule 1.7: Existing Clients May Present a Conflict of Interest

Rule 1.7 addresses the potential for conflicts of interest to occur when an attorney's representation of a client is jeopardized by other commitments or interests that compete with one another. The rule is essential to ensuring that lawyers continue to provide undivided devotion and loyalty to their respective clients:

"(a) A lawyer shall not represent a client if the representation involves a concurrent conflict of interest, save as allowed in paragraph (b), which states that a lawyer may represent a client if the representation involves a contemporaneous conflict of interest.

(1) the representation of one client will have an effect that is directly detrimental to the representation of another client; or

(2) there is a strong danger that the representation of one or more clients will be materially limited by the lawyer's responsibilities to another client, a former client, or a third person or by the lawyer's personal interest in the matter."

"(b) A lawyer may represent a client even if there is a concurrent conflict of interest as described in paragraph (a), provided that the following conditions are met:

(1) the attorney has a good faith belief that he or she will be able to represent each impacted client in an able and conscientious manner;

(2) the representation does not violate any legal restrictions;

(3) the representation does not involve the assertion of a claim by one client against another client represented by the lawyer in the same lawsuit or other

proceeding before a tribunal; and (4) the representation does not involve the lawyer's own participation in the litigation or other proceeding.

(4) Every customer who was impacted grants their informed consent, which is documented in writing.

Principal Components of Rule 1.7:

Definition of Conflict of Interest A conflict of interest occurs when a lawyer represents one client in a manner that is directly adverse to the interests of another client, or when there is a significant risk that the lawyer's ability to represent one or more clients will be materially limited by the lawyer's responsibilities to another client, a former client, or a third person.

Representation That Is Both Competent and Diligent Lawyers are permitted to continue with a representation that involves a conflict of interest if they have a reasonable belief that they can represent each affected client in a manner that is both competent and diligent.

In the event that there is a conflict of interest, each client who is affected must give their informed consent, which must then be acknowledged in writing. This must be done after the customer has been fully informed about the repercussions of the conflict.

Claim Representation That Is Prohibited In most cases, attorneys are not allowed to represent clients whose interests are in direct opposition to one another if the representation requires the presentation of a claim by one client against another client who is also being represented by the attorney in the same legal action or hearing before a tribunal.

Legal Restrictions: In order for the attorney to proceed with a case involving a conflict of interest, the representation in question cannot be against the law.

Rule 1.7 is absolutely necessary in order to maintain the level of confidence, fidelity, and undivided devotion that clients have come to expect from their attorneys. When addressing potential conflicts of interest, attorneys are required to act with prudence and transparency and acquire informed permission wherever it is appropriate.

Rule 1.8: Conflict of Interest: Specific Rules for Current Clients

Rule 1.8 of the Model Rules lays forth precise guidelines to follow when dealing with potential conflicts of interest with existing customers. This regulation tackles potential difficulties in the interaction between a lawyer and client and protects the rights of the client as follows:

"(a) A lawyer may not engage in commercial activity with a client or intentionally acquire an ownership, possessory, security, or other pecuniary interest that is adverse to a client unless one of the following conditions is met:

(1) the transaction and the terms on which the lawyer obtains the interest are fair and reasonable to the client, and they are fully disclosed and conveyed in writing in a manner that the client is able to understand in a manner that is reasonable;

(2) the client is informed in writing of the desirability of seeking the advice of independent legal counsel on the transaction and is given a reasonable opportunity to do so; and (3) the client is provided a reasonable opportunity to seek the advice of independent legal counsel on the transaction.

(3) The client grants informed assent to the essential elements of the transaction and the lawyer's position in the transaction, including whether the lawyer is representing the client in the transaction, in a written document that is signed by the client.

"(b) A lawyer shall not use information relating to representation of a client to the disadvantage of the client unless the client gives informed consent, except as permitted or required by these Rules."

"(c) A lawyer shall not solicit any substantial gift from a client, including a testamentary gift, or prepare on behalf of a client an instrument giving the lawyer or a person related to the lawyer any substantial gift unless the lawyer or other recipient of the gift is related to the client. For purposes of this paragraph, related persons include a spouse, child, grandchild, parent, or other relative or individual with whom the lawyer or the client maintains a close, familial relationship."

"(d) Prior to the conclusion of representation of a client, a lawyer shall not make or negotiate an agreement giving the lawyer literary or media rights to a portrayal or account based in substantial part on information relating to the representation."

Principal Components of Rule 1.8:

Business Transactions with Clients Lawyers are not allowed to enter into a business transaction with a client or acquire any interest that is adverse to the client unless the transaction is fair and reasonable, fully disclosed in writing, and the client is given the opportunity to seek independent legal counsel and gives informed consent. Also, lawyers are not allowed to represent more than one client in a business transaction at a time.

Use of Client Information Lawyers are banned from utilizing information linked to the representation of a client to the prejudice of the client unless the client grants informed consent or unless the Model Rules enable or necessitate the use of the information in question.

Gifts from Clients: Lawyers are not allowed to produce gift instruments for themselves or related individuals, nor are they allowed to seek major gifts from clients, including testamentary gifts. Furthermore, lawyers are not allowed to solicit considerable gifts from clients. The phrase "related persons" refers to members of the lawyer's or client's family as well as other individuals who have a close familial connection to either party.

Literary or Media Rights: Lawyers are not permitted to create agreements for literary or media rights based on information relating to the representation of a client before the representation has come to an end, nor are they permitted to negotiate such arrangements.

Rule 1.8 lays out stringent criteria that must be adhered to in order to prevent conflicts of interest, business dealings that could put the client at a disadvantage, and the improper use of client information. These standards are in place to protect the honesty of the attorney-client relationship and make certain that the client's interests are not jeopardized in any way by the attorney's pursuit of his or her own interests.

Establishing a Solid Relationship Between You and Your Lawyer

In order to conduct an ethical, professional, and responsible legal practice, it is vital to have a solid relationship with one's client. The formation of a healthy attorney-client relationship is facilitated by adhering to the following set of principles and recommendations for best practices:

Communication That Is Both Open and Honest Attorneys owe it to their clients to communicate in a manner that is both open and honest. It is important that customers be kept up to date on the status of their cases, as well as any noteworthy developments or modifications.

Listening Actively Lawyers have a responsibility to actively listen to the problems, inquiries, and expectations of their clients. It is essential to offer successful representation that one fully comprehends the client's point of view.

Transparency: Lawyers should be upfront about fees and expenses, which includes explaining the rationale for charges and making sure that clients understand the financial aspects of the representation they are receiving.

Managing Expectations: Attorneys owe it to their clients to assist them in managing their expectations by providing explanations of the potential outcomes, risks, and uncertainties involved in a case. The pleasure of customers can be increased by setting realistic expectations.

Respect for the Autonomy of the Client It is imperative that attorneys respect and defend their client's autonomy. This includes giving clients the opportunity to make educated judgments about the legal concerns affecting them, even while the attorney is providing counsel.

The resolution of conflicts requires that attorneys put in place processes for resolving disagreements or clearing up misunderstandings with their clients. It is absolutely necessary, for the sake of keeping a pleasant connection, to find prompt and efficient solutions to problems.

Ethical Standards: It is absolutely necessary to uphold the highest ethical standards possible. The clients of lawyers anticipate that their attorneys will behave professionally, with honesty and integrity.

Education of the Client It is the responsibility of the lawyer to teach the client on the legal process, including the language and the procedures. Clients who are well informed are in a better position to participate actively in the process of their representation.

Regarding client confidentiality, attorneys are required to take any and all necessary precautions. Clients should not be concerned about their privacy when discussing sensitive matters with their attorneys.

Informed Consent It is important for attorneys to gain informed consent from their clients whenever it is required. This is especially important in circumstances involving potential conflicts of interest, fees, or important choices.

counsel That Is Competent Customers of law firms anticipate that the attorneys they hire will deliver counsel that is both competent and conscientious. In order to live up to this expectation, attorneys need to consistently expand both their legal knowledge and their legal skills.

Managing Client Expectations Lawyers have a responsibility to set their clients' expectations on the legal process and the possible outcomes in a manner that is both clear and reasonable. To ensure that a client is happy, it is essential to manage their expectations.

Regulation of the Legal Profession is the subject of Chapter 7.

The practice of law is governed by an intricate set of rules and regulations since the legal profession is a crucial component of the judicial system. In this chapter, we will investigate the various facets of the regulation of the legal profession. In particular, we will focus on the Model Rules of Professional Conduct, admission to the bar, discipline and ethics, as well as the function of legal organizations.

Generally Accepted Standards of Professional Conduct

The American Bar Association (ABA) is responsible for the development of the Model Rules of Professional Conduct, which are an essential component in the regulation of the legal profession in the United States. The rules in this document provide ethical guidelines for lawyers and direct how they should behave in a variety of professional contexts. Although the Model Rules do not have the force of law on their own, they serve as a model code that many states in the United States have accepted with minor alterations in order to establish ethical standards for lawyers that are legally enforceable in their respective jurisdictions.

The Model Rules include a wide variety of subjects, including the following:

Relationship with the Client The regulations offer direction on how to communicate with clients, how to set up fee arrangements, how to handle potential conflicts of interest, and how to keep client information confidential.

They define the ethical responsibilities of attorneys in their function as advocates in litigation, including openness toward the tribunal and impartiality to opposing parties. Advocate: They outline the ethical responsibilities of lawyers in their role as advocates in litigation.

Transactions with Individuals Who Are Not Clients The guidelines govern how attorneys should conduct themselves while interacting with third parties such as opposing counsel, witnesses, and individuals who are not represented by an attorney.

Law Firms and Associations: They offer guidelines for lawyers who are employed by law firms or associations, with an emphasis on supervisory obligations, the responsibilities of partners, and law firm names.

Recognizing the significance of the lawyer's function as a public servant, the Model Rules include provisions for the tasks that should be fulfilled by attorneys when they are holding public office or working for the government.

customers Are Provided with correct and Relevant Information Regarding Legal Services They provide advise on lawyer advertising and solicitation, making certain that customers are given information that is both correct and pertinent regarding legal services.

Integrity of the Profession The rules emphasize the significance of protecting the integrity of the legal profession by addressing issues such as misbehavior, disciplinary measures, and disbarment of attorneys.

They handle trust accounts, client property, and the responsibilities of lawyers when it comes to handling client assets. Client protection is another topic that is covered.

Diversity and Inclusion: Recognizing the significance of having equal opportunity and representation, certain judicial systems have enacted measures to encourage diversity and inclusion in the legal profession.

It is necessary for lawyers to adhere to the Model Rules in order to maintain ethical conduct and uphold the integrity of the legal profession. As there are differences across the states, legal practitioners need to be informed of the special rules that have been adopted in their particular jurisdiction.

Admission to the Legal Profession

The procedure that must be followed in order to become a member of the bar is an essential part of the regulatory framework for the legal profession. Admission requirements ensure that individuals entering the legal profession have the appropriate qualifications and character to effectively and ethically represent clients in a manner that is consistent with professional standards. In most cases, the procedure will consist of the following steps:

Educational Requirements: Prospective employees have to earn a Juris Doctor (JD) degree from a law school that has been officially recognized. Additionally, the completion of additional coursework or an apprenticeship in the legal field may be necessary in certain jurisdictions.

Examination for the Bar: Being admitted to the bar often necessitates having a passing score on the bar examination. Candidates are evaluated based on their understanding of the law, which may include state-specific legislation depending on the circumstances.

Evaluation of Character and Physical Fitness Candidates are required to undergo a character and fitness evaluation so that it may be determined whether or not they have a moral character and whether or not they are suitable to practice law. Checks of the applicant's criminal history, interviews, and references could all be part of this review.

Oath of Office Successful applicants frequently make a public commitment by swearing an oath of office, in which they affirm their intention to uphold the law as well as the ethical norms of the legal profession.

Continuing Legal Education (CLE): Lawyers are required to participate in continued professional development throughout their careers by completing a predetermined amount of hours in CLE classes. The standards for CLE can vary from jurisdiction to jurisdiction.

Reciprocity and Admission on Motion: Certain jurisdictions let lawyers who have been admitted in other states to be admitted in their jurisdiction either by reciprocity or on motion, which simplifies the admission process for experienced lawyers.

Not only is it important to ensure that prospective lawyers have the necessary skills and morals, but it is also essential for the protection of clients' best interests and the upkeep of the honorable reputation of the legal profession. It is possible for the specific requirements and procedures to differ from jurisdiction to jurisdiction; therefore, prospective lawyers should educate themselves with the rules that are relevant in their state.

Discipline and Ethical Considerations

The regulation of the legal profession centers on ethical behavior in the profession as well as professional accountability. Mechanisms meant to address professional misconduct and safeguard the interests of clients and the public are used by the legal community to ensure compliance with these standards, which are then enforced. The following are important components of both discipline and ethics:

Complaints and Grievances: Clients and other individuals who believe that a lawyer has engaged in unethical conduct are able to file complaints or grievances with the proper legal authority, which is most commonly the state bar association.

Investigations: When a complaint is received by a legal authority, that authority will immediately begin an investigation to discover whether or not the claims are true. During investigations, one option is to conduct interviews with the necessary parties and evaluate the associated documentation.

Actions That May Be implemented in Disciplinary Matters If it is determined that wrongdoing has occurred, disciplinary measures may be implemented. These actions might vary from a private reprimand to being suspended from practicing law or even being disbarred. The nature and extent of the infraction will determine the level of the consequence that will be imposed.

Ethical Codes: The ethical codes that govern the legal profession include the Model Rules of Professional Conduct. These ethical standards govern the legal profession. In their professional work, attorneys are expected to behave in accordance with these norms.

Client Protection Funds: There are client protection funds available in many different countries, and its purpose is to give restitution to clients who have suffered monetary losses as a result of lawyer wrongdoing.

Claims of Legal Malpractice Clients who believe that they have been harmed as a result of negligence or misconduct on the part of their lawyers have the ability to file claims of legal malpractice in the civil courts.

Committees for Professional Responsibility: These committees supervise the disciplinary procedure, making certain that attorneys accused of unethical behavior are afforded their right to due process and that the general public is safeguarded.

Ethics Helplines and assistance Numerous bar associations offer ethics helplines and assistance in order to assist attorneys in navigating difficult ethical situations and coming to well-informed conclusions.

Review by Peers: Some judicial systems make use of procedures known as "peer reviews," in which other attorneys analyze and provide recommendations regarding how to handle allegations of unethical behavior.

In addition to being a requirement under the law, ethical behavior is also an essential component in the process of preserving trust within the legal profession. In order to safeguard the general public and maintain the integrity of the legal profession, there are procedures for disciplinary action and ethical principles in place.

Institutions of the Law and Regulatory Bodies

The regulation of the legal profession is overseen by a number of different legal organizations, including the following:

American Bar Association (ABA): The American Bar Association is a preeminent national organization that is responsible for developing the Model Rules of Professional Conduct as well as providing lawyers and other legal professionals with tools and assistance.

State Bar Associations: It is usual for each state to have its own bar association, which is tasked with the responsibility of regulating attorneys practicing within its borders. In many cases, state bar associations are responsible for establishing and enforcing particular ethical guidelines as well as providing members with support.

Branch of the Judiciary: The Judiciary Branch is an essential component in the process of regulating the legal profession. As part of this process, the Judiciary Branch is responsible for rendering final decisions on disciplinary cases and supervising the administration of bar examinations.

Legal Aid and Pro Bono Organizations: These organizations contribute to the role of the legal profession to serve the public interest by providing access to legal services for people who are unable to afford legal representation.

Institutions of Legal Education Both law schools and other types of legal education institutions play a part in the process of educating students to be admitted to the bar. They provide the fundamental education as well as the background knowledge that is required for practicing law.

Authorities in Charge of Legal Licensing Legal licensing authorities are responsible for overseeing the process of admission to the bar and establishing the conditions necessary to practice law in a certain jurisdiction.

Examining Committees for the Bar: These committees are in charge of developing and overseeing the bar examination, which is an essential part of the admissions process.

Committees on Legal Ethics Ethics committees within bar associations provide counsel on ethical concerns and participate in the regulation of the conduct of attorneys.

Regulation of the Legal Profession: Current Obstacles and Emerging Trends

Regulation of the legal profession is confronted with a number of issues and continuous developments, including the following:

The application of technology in the practice of law raises a number of ethical questions, including those of client confidentiality, online safety, and the application of artificial intelligence to legal problems.

Diversity and Inclusion: In recent years, there has been a shift in emphasis within the legal profession toward the promotion of diversity and inclusion. This shift reflects the significance of equitable representation and opportunity.

Access to Justice: There is an increasing emphasis on expanding access to justice, as many individuals still encounter difficulties to obtaining legal assistance. This is due to the fact that there are less and fewer judges in the United States.

Lawyers are currently navigating ethical difficulties in a global environment, addressing questions relating to cross-border legal practice and international legal ethics. This can be viewed as an example of the globalization of legal ethics.

Legal Education Reform In order to better prepare law students for the ever-changing legal landscape, legal education institutions are reevaluating and modifying the curriculums that they teach law students.

Innovating Regulation Some jurisdictions are looking into novel ways to regulate the legal industry, such as letting non-attorneys perform certain legal services or establishing new classifications of licensed legal professionals.

The necessity of addressing problems relating to mental health, maintaining a healthy work-life balance, and abusing substances is being increasingly recognized, and this has led to an increase in efforts to improve lawyer well-being.

Conflicts of Interest is the topic of Chapter 8.

In the field of law, conflicts of interest are a prevalent and complicated problem that can involve a range of different ethical, professional, and legal considerations. Conflicts can impair a lawyer's fiduciary obligation to operate in the best interests of their clients and have the potential to lead to unethical behavior, malpractice claims, disciplinary action, and unfavorable legal outcomes. Lawyers have a duty of fiduciary responsibility to their clients to act in their clients' best interests. In this chapter, we go deeply into the multifarious concept of conflicts of interest, investigating its definition, types, origins, and repercussions, as well as the ethical and legal frameworks for managing and minimizing conflicts.

Concerning the Definition of Conflicts of Interest

When a lawyer's personal, financial, or professional interests, or their commitments to other clients, third parties, or an organization, interfere with their capacity to represent a client in a diligent, loyal, and competent manner, this is considered to be a conflict of interest in the legal profession. These disagreements are possible at a number of points throughout the relationship between the client and the attorney, beginning with the consultation and continuing all the way through to the termination of the representation.

Conflicts of Interest Can Take Many Forms

There are three primary categories that can be used to classify conflicts of interest:

A conflict between clients arises when an attorney represents many clients whose interests are in conflict with one another or are in direct opposition to one another. There are two distinct varieties:

Direct conflicts are those that occur when the representation of one client is directly adverse to the representation of another client, such as when two clients involved in a commercial dispute have conflicting claims. Direct conflicts can also be referred to as unfavorable relationships.

Conflicts of material limitation emerge when there is a significant danger that the representation of one or more clients will be constrained by the lawyer's responsibilities to another client, a former client, a third party, or the lawyer's own interests. Conflicts of material limitation can also occur when there is a significant risk that the lawyer's own interests will be compromised.

Conflict Between the Lawyer and the Client This conflict may involve the personal, financial, or professional interests of the lawyer, which may limit their capability to represent the client in a diligent and loyal manner. For instance, if a lawyer has a financial interest in the verdict of a lawsuit they are representing a client in, this could compromise their objectivity.

Conflict Between an Attorney and a Former Client An attorney owes continued duties of secrecy and loyalty to former clients even after the attorney's relationship with the client has ended. It is possible for there to be a conflict of interest if the current client that a lawyer is representing has interests that are in opposition to those of a former client, or if the current client's representation requires the use of sensitive information obtained from the former client.

Reasons why people have competing interests

Many different things can give rise to conflicts of interest, including the following:

When an attorney represents many clients in the same case, there is a greater chance that there may be conflicts, particularly if the clients' interests are at odds with one another. This is referred to as dual or multiple representation.

Personal Interests It's not uncommon for attorneys to have personal financial or non-financial interests that compete with their ethical obligation to work in their clients' best interests. For instance, a lawyer may have a personal connection to one of the parties involved in a case or may have a financial interest in the outcome of the case.

Previous and present customers: Relationships with former and existing customers can give rise to a variety of disagreements. When an attorney has previously worked for a client, it can be difficult for them to take on a new client whose interests are in direct opposition to those of the previous client.

Organizational Conflicts It is possible for lawyers who represent organizations, such as companies or non-profits, to come across situations in which the interests of the organization and those of its individual executives, employees, or shareholders are in direct competition with one another.

Interference from Third Parties Conflicts can also develop from the involvement of third parties, such as insurance companies or co-counsel, who may attempt to exert influence on the decision-making process of the lawyer.

The Repercussions of Having Conflicting Interests

It is possible to incur major ethical and legal repercussions if conflicts of interest are not identified and addressed when they arise. The following are some of the possible repercussions:

Violations of Ethical Standards Lawyers who fail to resolve potential conflicts of interest may be in violation of ethical norms, such as those included in the Model norms of Professional Conduct. If this occurs, the state bar organization may take disciplinary action against the lawyer.

Loss of Trust and Credibility: Both clients and the general public anticipate that attorneys will behave in an honest and loyal manner. The exposure of a lawyer's conflicts of interest can wreak havoc on their professional reputation and erode client trust.

Claims of Legal Malpractice: Clients who believe that they have been harmed as a result of their lawyer's conflicts of interest may initiate legal malpractice claims, which may result in the lawyer being held financially liable for the damages.

Disqualification from Representation The courts have the authority to prevent attorneys from defending their clients in a particular case if they deem that the integrity of the legal process is being compromised by conflicts of interest.

Conflicts of interest can make it difficult for a lawyer to offer effective representation for a client, which can result in bad legal outcomes. Conflicts of interest can also lead to ethical violations.

A Moral Compass for Handling Matters Involving Conflicts of Interest

The Model Rules of Professional Conduct serve as the primary foundation for the ethical framework that governs the management of conflicts of interest; nevertheless, there are variances between jurisdictions. The resolution of conflicts is largely dependent on the following Model Rules:

Rule 1.7: Existing Clients May Present a Potential Conflict of Interest: According to this rule, a lawyer is not allowed to represent a client if doing so would create a concurrent conflict of interest. This rule applies when the lawyer's representation of one client would be directly adverse to the interests of another client, or when there is a significant risk that the lawyer's responsibilities to another client, a former client, a third person, or the lawyer's own personal interests would materially limit the representation of the client. However, under some circumstances, attorneys are allowed to continue representing their clients if they have obtained informed consent from their clients who are being adversely affected and have a reasonable belief that they can give competent and diligent representation.

Rule 1.8: Existing Clients May Present a Conflict of Interest: Detailed Regulations: Rule 1.8 outlines the particular guidelines that must be adhered to in the event of a business transaction between a lawyer and a client, the utilization of confidential client information in a manner that is detrimental to the client, or the giving of gifts from clients to lawyers.

Rule 1.9: Conflict of Interest: past Client The purpose of Rule 1.9 is to handle conflicts of interest that may develop as a result of a lawyer's representation of a current client, which may involve the use of information gained from a past client.

Rule 1.10, Concerning Imputed Conflicts of Interest, tackles the Imputation of Conflicts Within Law Firms This rule tackles the imputation of conflicts that exist within law firms. If one of the lawyers in a firm has a conflict of interest, then that conflict is considered to exist for all of the lawyers in the firm. There are, however, allowances made for things like information barriers and screens.

Rule 1.13: Organization as Client Requires Lawyers to Act in the Best Interests of the Organization When representing organizations, lawyers are required to act in the best interests of the organization, and they are also required to address any conflicts that may arise between the interests of the organization and the interests of the organization's constituents (such as officers, employees, or shareholders).

Controlling and Reducing Instances of Conflict of Interest

In order to safeguard their clients and their own professional standing, lawyers have the responsibility to actively detect, address, and mitigate any conflicts of interest that may arise. Included here are some strategies for conflict management and reduction:

Checks for Conflicts Before taking on a new client or case, lawyers should make sure there won't be any potential conflicts of interest with their existing or previous clients by conducting checks for conflicts of interest.

Informed Consent: There are some instances in which attorneys are permitted to continue representing their clients if they first seek informed consent from the clients who will be affected. This consent needs to be confirmed in writing, and it needs to come with a detailed breakdown of how the disagreement will be resolved.

Screening is a process that can be implemented in legal firms to separate lawyers with potential conflicts of interest from situations in which those potential conflicts could lead to complications. Specifically, this involves erecting informational walls within the company.

Withdrawal: In the event that conflicts cannot be resolved or are insurmountable, it may be necessary for attorneys to withdraw from representing a client in order to avoid violating professional ethics.

employing Specialized Counsel: In difficult situations, employing specialized counsel for various elements of a case can help to reduce the likelihood of conflicts occurring.

Conflict Waivers: The use of conflict waivers can be a helpful method for documenting the permission of affected clients in situations where informed consent is acquired.

The Very Best Methods for Attorneys
In order for lawyers to negotiate conflicts of interest in a way that is both successful and ethical, they need to adhere to best practices, such as the following:

Conduct Thorough Conflict Checks Before Taking on New Clients or Cases
You should always conduct thorough conflict checks before taking on new clients or cases. Make use of technological tools and databases to locate prospective points of contention.

contact: Make sure to keep an open line of contact with your customers regarding any potential problems that may arise and the steps you take to solve them.

Keep a record of everything: Maintaining in-depth records of conflict checks, client conversations, and conflict waivers is one way to show that you are diligent and transparent.

Training on a Regular Basis: To achieve compliance, it is important to maintain a current knowledge of ethical principles and to undergo training on a regular basis on potential conflicts of interest.

speak Colleagues: Whenever you are unsure about how to manage potential conflicts, it is best to speak with colleagues or ethics committees for help.

Billing That Is Open And Honest: When dealing with situations that involve disagreements, you need to make sure that the billing and fee arrangements are open and honest, and you should also document any fee sharing that may occur between attorneys.

Competence and Legal Misconduct is the Topic of Chapter 9.

law expertise is important to the successful operation of a law practice. In order to offer their clients with adequate representation, it is expected of lawyers that they possess the requisite knowledge, skills, and level of diligence. On the other hand, legal malpractice may take place when attorneys fail to live up to these standards, which may result in ethical and legal repercussions. In this chapter, we investigate the idea of competence in the legal profession, as well as the ethical duty that it imposes on lawyers, the causes that might lead to incompetence, and the legal malpractice claims that can emerge from failures in competence.

Gaining an Understanding of Legal Capability

Legal competence, which is also frequently referred to as professional competence, is the essential prerequisite for engaging in legal practice. It refers to the ability of a lawyer to provide legal services with the knowledge, competence, thoroughness, and preparation that are reasonably required for effective representation. Rule 1.1 of the Model Rules of Professional Conduct, which have been adopted by the majority of states in the United States, establishes the ethical obligation of competence:

"Competence: A lawyer's obligation to a client is to provide competent representation." To provide competent representation, one must have the legal expertise, technical know-how, level of detail, and level of preparation that are reasonably essential for the representation.

Components Essential to Competence:

Legal Knowledge In order to practice law successfully, attorneys need to have a solid understanding of the applicable laws, regulations, and legal principles. A thorough understanding of the law requires not only an understanding of substantive law but also of procedural regulations and the ability to undertake legal research.

Ability: In order to properly apply their legal knowledge, lawyers need to have the required abilities in their toolkit. This requires legal analysis, the ability to solve problems, the ability to negotiate, the ability to advocate, and other abilities pertinent to the particular legal case.

Attention to Detail: Being competent in legal work necessitates that you pay attention to detail. In order to give a comprehensive representation, attorneys are required to explore and analyze legal issues with diligence, read over and prepare papers, and pay careful attention to the details.

Preparation is essential, and attorneys have a duty to fully prepare for any case or other subject that they take on. In order to accomplish this, you will need to collect and organize evidence, conduct interviews with witnesses, and devise a plan for your representation.

Inability to fulfill these standards of competence can result in accusations of legal malpractice, disciplinary action by the state bar, and unfavorable legal outcomes for clients.

The Contributing Factors That Lead to Incompetence

Incompetence in the legal profession can be caused by a number of different events and situations, including the following:

Inexperienced lawyers may lack the required knowledge and abilities to provide adequate representation because they have not had the opportunity to practice law. Even though new lawyers frequently face a steep learning curve, it is nevertheless required of them to put in the effort necessary to acquire the necessary level of competence.

Overload and burnout: The ability of a lawyer to offer competent counsel may be compromised if the attorney takes on an overwhelming workload, works long hours without proper rest, or both. Errors and failures in judgment are both possible outcomes of fatigue.

Inability to Stay Current with Changing Legal Developments Because the law does not remain unchanged over time, attorneys are required to remain current with changing legal developments, including statutes, regulations, and case law. It is possible to become incompetent if this is not done.

Personal Issues The capacity of a lawyer to practice law competently might be hindered by personal issues such as health problems, financial challenges, or emotional stress.

Cases in Which Lawyers Neglect Their Clients' affairs There are certain instances in which lawyers neglect their clients' affairs by neglecting to communicate with their clients, conduct adequate research, or take appropriate action in a timely manner.

Lack of Ethical Conduct: Ethical infractions, such as conflicts of interest or breaches of confidentiality, might be taken as an indication of incompetence in understanding and adhering to ethical obligations.

Inadequate Communication Incompetence can arise from a failure to communicate adequately with clients, opposing parties, or the court. To be effective as attorneys, lawyers need to be able to communicate clearly, answer quickly to questions, and deliver arguments persuasively.

Abuse of the Legal System

Malpractice in the legal profession happens when an attorney violates their duty of competence, thereby putting their client in jeopardy. Clients allege that their attorneys' mistakes or omissions in representation contributed to unfavorable legal outcomes or financial losses when they bring cases alleging legal malpractice. Generally speaking, in order to establish a claim for legal malpractice, clients are required to prove the following elements:

As a result of the attorney-client relationship, the legal counsel had the responsibility to provide the client with competent representation.

Breach of Duty: The attorney did not meet the standard of competence in the same or similar circumstances, either via errors, omissions, or negligence. This might be considered a breach of duty.

The violation of the attorney's ethical obligations by the client was the direct cause of the client's suffering or loss. The client is required to demonstrate that a different conclusion would have been likely if not for the carelessness of the lawyer.

Damages: Customers have an obligation to demonstrate that they have suffered actual losses as a direct result of their attorney's ineptitude. These damages can take the form of monetary losses, legal repercussions, or any number of other undesirable events.

Varieties of Misconduct in the Legal System

Misconduct in the legal profession can take several forms, including the following:

The most typical reason for filing a claim for legal malpractice is negligence, which was committed by the defendant. It is possible for there to be mistakes, omissions, or a lack of proper attention in the portrayal, all of which can lead to this issue.

In breach of their fiduciary obligation, lawyers are expected to represent their clients in a manner that is in their clients' best interests. Claims of malpractice can result from the breach of this responsibility, which could take the form of a conflict of interest.

Due of the potential for a conflict of interest, attorneys are not allowed to represent clients who have competing interests. Malpractice claims are a potential outcome of failing to detect and handle potential conflicts of interest.

Failure to Communicate properly Failing to communicate properly with clients, other parties, or the court can lead to claims of malpractice. A failure to communicate effectively may result in missing deadlines, inadequate filings, or other unfavorable outcomes.

Errors in method Errors in the legal method, such as missing filing deadlines, can be considered negligent legal representation and constitute malpractice. These mistakes can lead to the forfeiture of legal rights or the removal of a case from consideration.

It is possible for attorneys to be held accountable for malpractice if they do not have adequate understanding of the law or if they do not correctly apply the law when representing a client in a legal matter.

Neglecting to Conduct an Investigation Lawyers have a responsibility to conduct investigations and acquire evidence whenever it is deemed to be reasonably required to do so. If you don't do that, you could end yourself facing malpractice lawsuits based on the fact that you weren't adequately prepared.

Defenses Available in Cases Involving Legal Misconduct

When confronted with allegations of legal malpractice, attorneys have the option of using a variety of defenses to push back against the accusations, including the following:

Lack of Causation: Attorneys may try to argue that the client's damages were not caused by their incompetence but rather by other causes or by the conduct of the client themselves.

It is possible for attorneys to argue that they did not owe their client a duty of care since there was no attorney-client relationship in place at the time.

No Violation: Attorneys might contest the allegation that they violated their duty of competence by arguing that they performed their duties with the utmost diligence and expertise.

The term "contributory negligence" refers to the practice of lawyers arguing that their client's acts or negligence contributed to the result that was unfavorable.

Claims for legal malpractice often have to be submitted within the allotted amount of time, which is governed by the statute of limitations. It is possible for attorneys to argue that the client's claim cannot be pursued because the statute of limitations has run out.

Avoiding Unprofessionalism in the Legal Profession

Lawyers have the ability to prevent claims of legal malpractice and ensure that they remain competent by taking the following preventative measures:

Continuing Education: It is important for attorneys to participate in ongoing legal education so that they can keep up with developments in the law and improve their abilities.

Effective communication with customers requires keeping lines of communication open, being truthful with them, and doing it on a consistent basis. The client's concerns should be swiftly addressed, clear expectations should be defined, and updates should be provided.

Avoiding Overload Attorneys should carefully manage their caseloads to prevent themselves from becoming overworked and burned out, which can result in errors and incompetence on their part.

Complete Documentation It is essential to maintain comprehensive records of all interactions with clients, as well as research and case work, in order to demonstrate diligence and expertise.

Adherence to Ethical Standards Lawyers are expected to adhere to high ethical standards, which include avoiding conflicts of interest and protecting the confidentiality of their clients.

Mentoring and Supervision: In order to increase their level of expertise, newly licensed attorneys should seek out mentoring and direction from more seasoned colleagues or supervisors.

The client-attorney privilege and confidentiality are the topics covered in Chapter 10.

The attorney-client relationship and the legal profession place a high premium on keeping client information private and maintaining the privilege of attorney-client privilege. In addition to being reinforced by legal laws and privileges that guarantee the confidentiality and trust that are inherent in this relationship, these principles have their origins in the ethical commitment that lawyers have to their clients to keep their clients' information private. In the following chapter, we will discuss the ideas of secrecy and attorney-client privilege, as well as their ethical and legal underpinnings, the scope of their protection, and the exceptions and restrictions that are associated with each notion.

Maintaining privacy within the attorney-client relationship is of the utmost importance.

Relationship Between Attorney and Client The relationship between an attorney and a client is one of the most basic aspects of the legal profession. It is predicated on trust, confidence, and the assumption that clients can communicate openly and honestly with their attorneys regarding any and all matters pertaining to their cases. Lawyers have a responsibility to work in the clients' best interests, to defend their clients' rights, and to represent their clients with vigorous advocacy.

Duty of Confidentiality The duty of confidentiality owed by the lawyer is one of the most important aspects of this partnership. Rule 1.6 of the Model Rules of Professional Conduct states that it is the responsibility of lawyers to maintain the confidentiality of all information concerning their clients. This responsibility extends to any and all information that is relevant to the representation, regardless of whether the material was produced by the client or the attorney.

The duty of confidentiality extends to include all client communications, legal strategies, advice, and records. The scope of confidentiality includes all of these things. Attorneys are obligated to take all precautions necessary to prevent this information from being shared with unintended parties.

Duration of the responsibility to Maintain Confidentiality The responsibility to maintain confidentiality does not end when the connection between the attorney and client does. It is a commitment that lasts a lifetime and extends to previous customers. The confidentiality of their former clients' information must be maintained at all times by legal professionals.

Justifications for Maintaining Confidentiality: Maintaining privacy is necessary for a number of reasons, including the following:

It encourages clients to submit their lawyers with information that is complete as well as honest.

It helps to cultivate trust in the relationship between the client and the attorney.

It enables attorneys to deliver sound advice to their clients and to passionately advocate on their behalf, both of which contribute to more effective legal representation.

It safeguards the clients' legal rights by preventing the information they provide from being utilized in a manner that is detrimental to them.

There are some exemptions to the obligation to maintain confidentiality.

Even though the duty of secrecy is extremely broad, there are certain situations in which attorneys are permitted or even required to reveal information about their clients. The following are some examples of common exceptions:

Informed Consent: If a client gives an attorney informed consent, the lawyer is allowed to reveal sensitive material. It is imperative that this be carried out with the client's complete and unqualified assent at all times.

For the sake of protecting others, attorneys are permitted to reveal client confidences if doing so will prevent their client from committing a crime that could result in serious bodily injury or even death. Having said that, this exemption is read in a very restrictive manner.

In the event that it is absolutely necessary, lawyers may provide client information in order to defend themselves against legal malpractice claims that have been brought by their clients.

In order for attorneys to fulfill their other legal responsibilities, such as obeying court orders, responding to subpoenas, or abiding by ethical standards, it is possible that they will be obliged to reveal information. However, they should make a good faith effort to restrict the information disclosed to only that which is necessary.

Obtaining Legal Advice In order to avoid breaching client confidentially when seeking legal advice or ethical direction, lawyers may consult with one another in the profession.

Privilege between an Attorney and a Client

The following is a definition of privilege: The attorney-client privilege is a legal concept that prevents confidential communications between a client and their lawyer from being revealed in the course of a legal procedure. This privilege preserves the client's right to privacy. Because of this, clients are able to speak candidly with their attorneys, safe in the assurance that the content of their conversations will not be disclosed.

Components That Make Up the Attorney-Client Privilege:

Communication That Is Kept Confidential The conversation needs to be kept confidential, which means that its participants should keep it to themselves and not share it with anyone else.

Communication Ought to Take Place Between the Lawyer and the Client or Their Agents When it comes to the facilitation of legal counsel, communication ought to take place between the lawyer and the client or their agents.

For the Purpose of Seeking or Receiving Legal assistance: The communication needs to be made for the purpose of trying to find or get legal assistance.

The Protected Areas of the Attorney-Client Relationship:

The attorney-client privilege protects a wide variety of conversations between attorneys and their clients, including verbal, written, and electronic exchanges as well as other forms of contact.

The privilege applies to conversations with the lawyer's agents, such as paralegals and legal secretaries, who are required to aid the provision of legal advice.

It is possible for it to preserve communications made during the attorney-client relationship as well as communications made after the relationship has ended.

With the following exceptions and restrictions:

Communication between an attorney and a client that is made with the intent to commit a crime or defraud another person is not protected by the attorney-client privilege.

If a customer freely discloses confidential information to third parties, the privilege associated with that information may be lost.

In most cases, the privilege does not apply if the client seeks legal assistance in order to further an ongoing crime or fraud, or to commit one in the future.

When a client puts their communications with their lawyer into question during a legal procedure, the client may relinquish the privilege that normally exists between the attorney and the client.

Disclosure of Attorney-Client Confidential Information:

Waiver can take place if the client voluntarily discloses the privileged information to a third party or if the client places the privileged information "at issue" in a legal case. Both of these scenarios are examples of situations in which a client may waive their privileges.

It is imperative for attorneys to exercise extreme caution so as not to mistakenly waive client privilege and to take active measures to safeguard their clients' personal information.

The Work Product Doctrine states that.

The work product doctrine is a form of related protection that applies to items that have been generated by attorneys in preparation for potential legal action.

With a few notable exceptions, it gives attorneys the ability to keep their notes, tactics, and analyses secret during the course of court procedures.

Representation in Joint Capacity and Waiver:

If a lawyer represents many clients at the same time, those clients may choose to forgo the attorney-client privilege with regard to one another. This may occur if their interests are in direct opposition to one another.

When numerous clients are being represented jointly by one attorney, the attorney is required to tell all of the clients about the possibility of a waiver.

Concerning Potential Conflicts of Interest and Maintaining Confidentiality:

In order to protect their clients' right to confidentiality and the attorney-client privilege, lawyers have a responsibility to handle any conflicts of interest that may arise in their practices.

Because conflicts of interest can give rise to ethical conundrums, attorneys are required to take precautions in order to safeguard the interests and sensitive information of all of their clients.

In the context of the corporation: privilege

The attorney-client privilege can be difficult to navigate in the business world since it may encompass conversations between attorneys, corporate officers, employees, and even members of the board of directors of the corporation.

It is critical for businesses to institute policies and protocols that safeguard privileged communications and delineate the differences between legal and non-legal advice.

Fraud and Criminal Activity Exception:

There is an exemption to the attorney-client privilege known as the crime-fraud exception. This exception permits the revelation of communications that would normally be protected from public view if they were made in furtherance of a crime or fraud.

There is a possibility that attorneys have a professional obligation to provide such information in order to put a stop to or correct the fraudulent activity.

Myths That Are Widespread Regarding the Attorney-Client Privilege:

Protection Without Limits or Exceptions The attorney-client privilege does not provide complete protection because it is subject to certain exceptions and restrictions.

Protection of All Client Information The attorney-client privilege does not provide blanket protection for all information pertaining to a client. It is necessary that the communication fulfill certain requirements.

Protection Against All Disclosures: The attorney-client privilege might not be able to prevent disclosure in all situations, such as when there are criminal investigations going on or when certain government inquiries are being conducted.

Problems that arise in the age of digital technology:

The protection of attorney-client privilege and confidentiality in the modern day faces additional issues as a result of the rise of digital technology. The possibility of electronic spying, hacking, and data breaches is something that all lawyers need to be aware of.

When it comes to protecting client confidentiality, using secure communication channels and encryption is becoming increasingly vital.

Conflicts in the Legal Profession is the topic of Chapter 11.

The term "conflicts in the legal profession" refers to a wide variety of ethical, professional, and interpersonal concerns that might emerge during the course of legal practice. These conflicts may entail ethical quandaries, the interests of clients, personal ideals, or obligations to the court. In this chapter, we will discuss the many different forms of conflicts that lawyers face, the ethical and professional principles that govern disputes, as well as ways for effectively identifying, managing, and resolving conflicts.

Conflicts in the Legal Profession: An Overview and Introduction

Given the numerous responsibilities that attorneys play in fighting for their clients, enforcing the law, and resolving complicated ethical challenges, conflicts in the legal profession are inherent to the practice of law. This is especially true given the nature of the profession itself. The following are the three primary categories into which these disputes can be placed:

Ethical Conflicts: Ethical conflicts encompass conundrums relating to professional conduct, the responsibility of loyalty to clients, and the observance of ethical principles. If a client wants an attorney to pursue a legal strategy that may be legally permitted but ethically questionable, for instance, the attorney may find themselves in a position where they are faced with an ethical dilemma.

Interest Conflicts: Interest conflicts occur when a lawyer's personal or financial interests may clash with their duty to act in the best interests of their clients.

These conflicts might arise when a client hires a lawyer to represent their best interests. This includes financial conflicts, conflicts connected to personal relationships with opposing parties or witnesses, and conflicts related to other clients or third parties.

Conflicts of Jurisdiction Dealing with conflicts of jurisdiction requires being aware of and able to navigate differences in the laws, regulations, and ethical standards that apply in several jurisdictions. This is something that is especially important for attorneys who work in a number of different states or worldwide.

Ethical Principles That Guide Conflict Resolution

Lawyers are required to abide by a set of ethical guidelines that handle potential conflicts of interest and provide direction for how they should behave in order to uphold the honor of the legal profession and the confidence of the general public. These guidelines offer a structure for locating potential points of contention, developing strategies for dealing with them, and, if required, finding solutions to them.

Model principles of Professional Conduct The Model Rules of Professional Conduct published by the American Bar Association are used as a fundamental reference for ethical principles guiding conflicts in the United States. Although different states may adopt somewhat different versions of these standards, in general they comply with the Model standards.

Concerning Potential Conflicts of Interest, the Model Rules Have a Rule Number One Point One Point Seven. It prevents attorneys from representing a client when there is a concurrent conflict of interest between the attorney and the client. If the representation of one client is directly adverse to the representation of another client, or if there is a significant risk that the representation will be materially limited by the lawyer's responsibilities to another client, a former client, a third person, or the lawyer's own personal interests, this is considered to be a concurrent conflict of interest.

Informed Consent: In accordance with Rule 1.7, attorneys are permitted to continue with representation even in the midst of a conflict of interest provided that they receive informed consent from all of the clients who would be impacted by the representation. This consent ought to be verified in writing, and it ought to include a crystal clear explanation of the disagreement and its repercussions.

Confidentiality and Conflicts of Interest: Rule 1.6 of the Model Rules emphasizes how important it is to safeguard the confidentiality of client information. Even in the face of potential conflicts, attorneys are obligated to protect their clients' confidentiality in order to keep their clients' faith in them and protect their right to personal space.

This rule provides particular restrictions relating to conflicts of interest between lawyers and clients, including business transactions, use of client information, and taking gifts from clients. Model Rule 1.8: This rule outlines specific requirements connected to conflicts of interest between lawyers and clients.

Imputed Conflicts: Rule 1.10 handles imputed conflicts, which occur when disputes that arise inside a law firm can be attributed to all of the firm's lawyers. On the other hand, there are several exemptions made for screens and other information obstacles that hinder imputation.

Model Rule 1.9 tackles potential conflicts of interest with past customers and places an emphasis on the continuous duty of maintaining confidentiality and loyalty to former customers.

Conflicts of various kinds that might arise in the legal profession

Client disputes are disagreements that arise between individuals who are represented by the same attorney or law firm. It is imperative that attorneys steer clear of scenarios in which they are forced to represent clients whose respective interests are in direct opposition to one another.

Personal conflicts can arise for lawyers when their personal interests or relationships have the potential to interfere with their professional commitments to clients. Personal conflicts can also arise when a client's case is emotionally charged. For instance, a personal conflict may arise when an attorney has a personal relationship with a party that they are representing in court.

Financial Conflicts: Financial conflicts occur when a lawyer's financial interests, such as investments or commercial transactions, interfere with their obligation to act in the best interests of a client. Financial conflicts can emerge when a lawyer's financial interests conflict with their duty to act in the best interests of a client. The interests of their clients should always come first for lawyers; they should never engage in self-dealing.

Conflicts Involving Third Parties A lawyer may find themselves in a situation where a conflict involves a third party, such as a dispute between a current or former client, a witness, or a co-counsel. It is the responsibility of attorneys to effectively handle and address these issues.

Conflicts of Jurisdiction: Conflicts of jurisdiction can arise when attorneys practice law in many states or worldwide, requiring them to navigate variances in the laws, regulations, and ethical standards that apply in each jurisdiction.

Conflict Prevention, Management, and Resolution in the Legal Profession

The legal profession relies heavily on effective conflict management in order to uphold high levels of ethical and professional standards. In order to successfully detect, manage, and resolve conflicts, legal professionals and law firms should develop and implement appropriate procedures and guidelines.

Checks for any Conflicts of Interest Before agreeing to represent new clients or cases, legal professionals are expected to perform exhaustive checks for any conflicts of interest. In order to discover potential conflicts, this requires exploring databases, evaluating case histories, and speaking with peers.

permission That Is Informed When there are potential conflicts of interest that might be avoided by obtaining the client's informed permission, lawyers owe it to their impacted clients to explain the nature of the conflict and its repercussions. Consent from customers must be provided in writing.

Screening processes: Lawyers in law firms have the ability to implement screening processes in order to separate conflicted lawyers from situations in which those lawyers' conflicts could potentially cause problems. Establishing information barriers is necessary in order to stop the attribution of internal conflicts within the company.

Withdrawal from Representation: In situations where conflicts are either impossible to manage or cannot be avoided, it may be necessary for lawyers to withdraw from representing their clients in order to avoid violating professional ethics.

Outside Counsel or Co-Counsel: When dealing with complicated cases that involve disputes, attorneys may want to seek the assistance of outside counsel or co-counsel in order to address various areas of a case and to manage conflicts.

Guidance in Ethical Matters When attorneys are unsure how to handle a conflict, they should seek advice from their colleagues, ethics committees, or bar associations. This is an ethical best practice.

Regarding the maintenance of secrecy, attorneys are obligated to guarantee that all pertinent information is shielded from public view while simultaneously managing and resolving disputes.

Methodologies for the Resolution of Ethical Conflicts:

The key to transparency is maintaining open and honest contact with customers. The conflict, its potential impact, and the means by which it will be managed or resolved should be explained by the attorneys.

Alternative Representation: In certain circumstances, the lawyer could be required to suggest that the client with the conflict speak with another attorney.

Arbitration or Mediation: In situations involving client disagreements, either mediation or arbitration may prove to be an efficient technique of resolving the problem.

Court Intervention: In certain circumstances, a court may be required to intervene in order to resolve problems. One example of this is when two clients have interests that are directly in conflict with one another.

Consent and Waiver: Customers might agree to continue with representation despite potential conflicts of interest if informed consent and waivers are obtained. However, this strategy calls for extreme caution while being implemented.

Different Functions of a Lawyer Presented in Chapter 12

Advocates, counselors, negotiators, and mediators are just some of the functions that lawyers perform in society; other responsibilities include conflict resolution, negotiation, and more. In addition to representing clients in court and conducting legal research, their responsibilities also encompass other activities that are crucial to the operation of a fair and well-governed society. In this chapter, we discuss the many responsibilities that come with being a lawyer, such as being an advocate, a counselor, a problem solver, and more. In addition to this, we will talk about the ethical issues, duties, and difficulties that are involved with each function.

1. The Supporting Party

Perhaps the aspect of a lawyer's job that is most known to the general public is that of an advocate. In the course of legal proceedings, whether they take place in a courtroom or some other type of conflict resolution environment, advocacy entails representing and supporting the interests of clients. A few examples of advocacy are:

Representing clients in legal processes before a judge, such as trials, hearings, and motions, is referred to as "litigation."

The process of attempting to achieve mutually beneficial agreements for one's clients while negotiating with the other party or parties.

The process of assisting in the resolution of disputes by means of mediation, most commonly in the role of a mediator.

Arbitration entails either acting as an arbitrator or an advocate for clients during the course of arbitration proceedings.

Ethical Considerations Advocates have an ethical responsibility to zealously advocate their clients within the parameters of the law and ethical standards. They have a responsibility to tell the court and the opposing parties the truth, and they should avoid pursuing claims that are without merit.

Advocates are tasked with the responsibility of preparing cases, presenting evidence, making legal arguments, and cross-examining witnesses in order to further the interests of their clients.

Problems The adversarial nature of advocating can often lead to moral conundrums, such as weighing the obligation to aggressively represent a client against the obligation to be truthful with the court.

2. The Advisor to the Client

Lawyers frequently take on the role of counselors for their clients, advising them on how to handle various legal issues and assisting their customers in gaining a better understanding of their legal standing and available choices. Counselors have an important part to play in the following:

Legal counsel refers to the process of advising clients on their rights, duties, and possible courses of action in the event of a legal dispute.

Risk assessment refers to the process of evaluating the potential adverse legal consequences and advantageous opportunities presented by a variety of various techniques.

Preventative Measures Consist of Advising Clients on the Ways to Prevent Legal Problems and Mitigate Risks.

Ethical considerations dictate that counselors must present clients with advise that is both knowledgeable and honest, even if the client does not want to hear it. In addition to this, they should take into account the client's priorities and objectives.

Counselors have the responsibility of assisting clients in making educated decisions, navigating complex legal processes, and avoiding legal hazards.

It can be difficult to give counsel that is in the client's best interest while also respecting their autonomy and the decisions they make. This can be a challenge. Additionally, counselors are obligated to have a current knowledge of ever-evolving legal guidelines.

3. The One Who Finds Solutions

Lawyers frequently take on the role of problem-solvers, searching for answers to their clients' legal challenges that are both practical and inventive in nature. To solve a problem, you need to:

Helping to resolve issues through negotiation, mediation, arbitration, or any of the other ADR procedures is referred to as alternative dispute resolution, or ADR for short.

Transactional work includes drafting and negotiating contracts, mergers and acquisitions, and estate planning agreements, among other types of agreements, in order to accomplish the aims of the client.

Legal Research is the process of conducting in-depth research with the goal of locating answers to difficult legal topics.

Ethical Considerations Problem solvers have a responsibility to their clients to find solutions that are in their clients' best interests while also adhering to ethical rules and maintaining professional standards.

Problem solvers are required to have the knowledge and abilities necessary to analyze difficult legal problems, conduct research on possible solutions, and present these possibilities to their customers.

Achieving solutions through alternative dispute resolution (ADR) that are acceptable to both parties, drafting contracts that are specific and exhaustive, and doing exhaustive legal research can be challenging jobs.

4. The One Who Mediates

A neutral third person, known as the mediator, assists the parties in obtaining a conclusion that is acceptable to both of them during the dispute resolution process known as mediation. Lawyers frequently act as mediators, guiding the parties involved through the process of evaluating their choices and identifying areas of agreement.

Ethical considerations dictate that mediators maintain their objectivity and neutrality at all times, so as to guarantee a fair procedure for all involved parties. They are not permitted to offer the parties any form of legal advice.

Mediators' responsibilities include facilitating communication, encouraging cooperation, and assisting parties in identifying areas of shared interest and possible points of agreement.

obstacles The three most significant obstacles that mediators have are maintaining their neutrality, controlling their emotions, and assisting the parties in breaking down communication barriers.

5. The Person Who Teaches

The function of an educator is one that lawyers play by assisting their clients in comprehending the legal ramifications of their circumstances, their rights and obligations, as well as the potential outcomes that could result from the decisions that they make.

Ethical considerations require attorneys to give clients correct information and ensure that they are able to make judgments based on that knowledge.

Educators have the responsibility of answering clients' inquiries and explaining difficult legal ideas in language that is easy to understand.

The process of translating legal language into terms that clients can understand and addressing the concerns or emotional issues that their clients face can be challenging.

6. The Watchdog for Ethical Conduct

Lawyers play the role of ethical watchdogs by ensuring the highest ethical standards are met in the practice of law, maintaining their own high standards of professional conduct, and holding clients and colleagues accountable when ethics are violated.

Ethical Considerations: Lawyers have a responsibility to set a good example for their clients in terms of ethical conduct, to protect the confidentiality of their clients' information, and to report instances of unethical activity when they occur.

Ethical guardians have the responsibility to adhere scrupulously to ethical guidelines and to hold individuals accountable when such guidelines are broken by others.

Ethical challenges might arise when trying to strike a balance between the obligation to disclose unethical conduct and the obligation to maintain client confidentiality.

7. The Individual in Public Service

A number of attorneys choose to devote their professional lives to serving the public by taking jobs with government agencies, charitable organizations, or legal assistance organizations. They are an essential component in the administration of justice and the delivery of legal assistance to marginalized groups.

Ethical Considerations It is incumbent upon those entrusted with public duties and responsibilities to uphold ethical standards while carrying out those duties and responsibilities.

The responsibilities of public servants include the obligation to serve the public interest, the duty to preserve the rights of individuals, and the duty to guarantee that individuals have access to justice.

Problems It can be difficult to strike a balance between the demands of public service and the ethical requirements that come with it, especially the possibility of conflicts of interest.

8. The Proponent of the Policy

Policy advocacy is a common activity for lawyers, who frequently collaborate with legislators, policymakers, and advocacy groups in order to mold and exert influence over regulatory and legal frameworks.

Considerations Regarding Ethics Policy advocates are obligated to observe ethical standards and to preserve transparency in their advocacy efforts.

Policy advocates are responsible for conducting research and analysis of legal issues, developing legislative recommendations, and engaging in advocacy activities in order to advance the desired changes in laws and regulations.

It can be difficult to strike a balance between ardent advocacy and ethical conduct, and it can also be difficult to navigate the complicated world of legislative and regulatory processes. Both of these challenges can be difficult to overcome.

9. The Presiding Court Justice or Arbitrator

Some attorneys take on the role of judge or arbitrator in the various alternative dispute resolution systems that are available. They are accountable for ensuring that conflicts are resolved in a manner that is fair and just.

Ethical Considerations In order to preserve their independence and fairness, judges and arbitrators are expected to abide by a stringent set of ethical principles and standards.

Judges and arbitrators have the responsibility of presiding over cases, interpreting the law, and making decisions in a fair and impartial manner.

Maintaining objectivity while simultaneously managing difficult cases, enforcing the law, and ensuring that justice is served can be extremely difficult tasks.

10. The Pioneering Spirit

Lawyers are increasingly taking on the role of innovators in the fast evolving legal landscape. They are developing new technologies and methods to increase access to justice as well as the quality of legal services.

Ethical Considerations: Innovators have a responsibility to ensure that their inventions comply with ethical and legal norms and do not put the quality of legal services or their ethics at risk.

Innovators are responsible for conceptualizing and putting into action the technical solutions, legal platforms, and tools that improve the delivery of legal services by making them more effective and more easily available.

The challenges include striking a balance between the need to innovate and the need to comply with ethical and regulatory standards, addressing potential ethical conundrums posed by technological advancements, and ensuring that innovations help rather than hurt legal services.

Officials in the Judicial and Legal System, Chapter 13

The administration of justice, enforcing the law, and ensuring that the legal process runs smoothly are the responsibilities of judicial and legal authorities, who are considered to be significant players in the legal system. This chapter examines the functions and responsibilities of various judicial and legal authorities, such as judges, magistrates, clerks, court reporters, and other professionals who play important roles in the judicial and legal systems.

1. The Judiciary

Judges are essential members of the judicial system because they preside over court hearings, interpret the law, and hand down rulings. The following are some of their jobs and responsibilities:

Impartiality in Judgment Judges are tasked with the responsibility of ensuring that matters are heard in a manner that is both fair and impartial, applying the law to the circumstances at hand, and making decisions based on legal principles and precedences.

Judges are responsible for the management of the cases on their dockets, which includes the creation of schedules, the issuance of orders, and the supervision of both pre-trial and trial procedures.

The ability to interpret and clarify legal principles and statutes places them at the center of the process of creating legal precedents and the ongoing development of the law.

When it comes to sentencing, the factors and circumstances of each individual case are taken into consideration by the judges who preside over criminal trials.

Instructions to the Jury In trials that are conducted before juries, the judges give the jurors instructions regarding the applicable law and the legal norms.

Research in the Law Judges may be required to do research in the law so that they can better grasp difficult legal matters and make decisions based on accurate information.

2. Courts of Magistracy

Magistrates are court officers who have responsibility over a variety of different legal problems, including pre-trial proceedings and situations involving less serious offenses. The following are some of their jobs and responsibilities:

Pre-Trial Proceedings: Magistrates are in charge of handling pre-trial motions, evidence hearings, and discovery issues, all of which help to ensure that cases are managed effectively.

They promote settlement negotiations and mediations to resolve matters before they go to trial. Settlement Conferences.

Report and Recommendation Magistrates have the authority to present the presiding judge with reports and recommendations about particular aspects of the law.

Issuing Warrants Magistrates in some countries have the authority to issue search warrants and arrest warrants, and this varies from jurisdiction to jurisdiction.

3. Clerks of the several courts

Administrative specialists known as clerks of court are tasked with the management of court documents and proceedings, in addition to offering assistance to judges, attorneys, and members of the general public. The following are some of their jobs and responsibilities:

Clerks are responsible for the management of court dockets, scheduling, and record-keeping in order to ensure the smooth progression of cases through the court system.

Keeping Records: They are responsible for keeping records of court hearings, orders, judgments, and various other relevant papers.

Operations of the Clerk's Office Clerks are responsible for managing the daily operations of the clerk's office, which include filing documents, processing fees, and providing the public with information.

Jury Selection: In a number of legal systems, clerks play a role in both the selection of jurors and the management of jury pools.

4. Reporters who work in courts

The creation of verbatim transcripts of legal proceedings, such as court sessions, depositions, and other legal proceedings is the responsibility of court reporters. The following are some of their jobs and responsibilities:

Court reporters are responsible for recording and trancribing what is said in courtroom proceedings in order to produce an accurate written record of the proceedings.

Real-Time Reporting: Real-time reporting is a service that is provided by some court reporters. This service enables parties to access a transcript as it is being prepared.

Legal video services include video recording and deposition services, which are sometimes offered by court reporters.

5. The Bailiffs

The bailiffs are the law enforcement personnel who are tasked with the responsibility of keeping the courtroom secure and in order. The following are some of their jobs and responsibilities:

Bailiffs are responsible for ensuring the safety and security of the courtroom, as well as the judges, jurors, attorneys, and any other individuals who take part in court procedures.

Maintaining Order: They are in charge of maintaining decorum in the courtroom, which includes enforcing the rules of the court and making sure that all participants behave in a proper manner.

Assisting the Judge Bailiffs are able to assist the judge in a variety of ways, including distributing documents, operating courtroom equipment, and accompanying the judge as necessary.

6. Those Charged with Probation

Officers of the court who work with people who have been placed on probation or parole in order to monitor whether or not they are adhering to the conditions that were established by the court. The following are some of their jobs and responsibilities:

Probation officials are responsible for monitoring individuals who are on probation to ensure that they are adhering to the terms and conditions that were issued by the court.

Assessment: They evaluate the needs and risks of probationers and then provide referrals to suitable services such as counseling or job training as necessary.

Reports for the Court Probation officers are responsible for preparing reports for the court that detail the compliance and progression of a probationer.

When it comes to enforcement, probation officers have the authority to make recommendations to the court regarding suitable sanctions to impose on probationers who break the terms of their supervision.

7. Legal Counsel

Attorneys are specialists in the legal field who represent their clients in court and other legal proceedings. Their roles and responsibilities include a wide variety of legal responsibilities, including the following:

A client's interests are represented in court by their attorney, who argues the law on the client's behalf and advocates for the client's best interests.

Legal Research: In order to bolster their cases, they engage in legal research, which helps to ensure that their legal arguments are well-founded.

Client Counsel Attorneys are responsible for providing their clients with legal advice in order to assist their clients in better understanding both their rights and obligations.

Lawyers are responsible for negotiating settlements, plea bargains, and other types of legal agreements on their clients' behalf in the context of the negotiation process.

Litigation: They initiate legal actions, compile necessary paperwork, and argue their clients' issues before a judge.

8. Legal secretaries and assistants

Alongside attorneys, paralegals do tasks such as conducting research on legal issues, drafting relevant documents, and managing client cases. The following are some of their jobs and responsibilities:

Paralegals are responsible for conducting legal research in order to assist attorneys in the preparation of cases and the development of legal arguments.

Preparation of papers: They are responsible for the preparation of legal papers like pleadings, contracts, and legal memoranda.

Case Management Paralegals provide assistance in managing cases, which may include tasks such as organizing documents and client correspondence in addition to scheduling.

Interviews with Clients: In order to obtain information, they may conduct interviews with clients and witnesses.

9. Public Defenders and Legal Assistance Programs

People who cannot afford private legal representation are eligible for legal representation from public defenders and attorneys who work for legal aid organizations. The following are some of their jobs and responsibilities:

Representation: They represent their clients in a variety of legal matters, including family law, criminal law, and civil law.

Advocacy is the process by which legal aid and public defenders represent their clients' best interests and work to ensure that their clients are treated fairly and equally under the law.

Referrals to Resources: In order to help clients address non-legal concerns that are harming their wellbeing, they may direct clients to social services and support organizations.

10. Translators Working in the Courts

Interpreters in the courtroom play a crucial part in ensuring that individuals who do not understand English can communicate effectively with the judicial system. The following are some of their jobs and responsibilities:

Court interpreters translate both oral and written language for those who are not fluent in the language used in the court where they are being tried.

Accurate Interpretation: They make certain that those involved in the legal process thoroughly comprehend the proceedings and are able to interact with one another in an efficient manner.

Independence: Court interpreters are required to maintain their independence and refrain from offering any kind of legal advice or opinion.

11. Legal Professional Responsibility and Regulatory Bodies

Authorities in charge of legal ethics and disciplinary matters are the ones tasked with enforcing ethical standards within the legal profession and examining allegations of improper behavior on the part of attorneys. The following are some of their jobs and responsibilities:

These authorities ensure that ethical standards are adhered to by attorneys by enforcing norms of professional behavior and ensuring that lawyers follow the regulations.

Complaints Against Lawyers Are Looked Into They look into complaints lodged against lawyers, which could result in disciplinary action being taken in the event that misbehavior is discovered.

Education: Authorities on legal ethics may educate and advise lawyers on their ethical commitments and the most effective ways to fulfill those obligations.

12. Professors of Legal Studies

Law professors are educators who are responsible for teaching law students, contributing to the field of legal scholarship, and providing the community with legal expertise. The following are some of their jobs and responsibilities:

Teaching is the primary responsibility of law professors, who are responsible for educating students who will go on to become lawyers.

They contribute to the expansion of legal knowledge by doing research in the legal field and publishing articles and books on subjects related to the law.

Participation in the Community Law professors may provide their legal expertise to the community by way of pro bono work or by acting as expert witnesses.

13. People Who Do Research in the Law

Legal researchers are responsible for doing exhaustive research to support legal proceedings, academic work, or the creation of public policy. The following are some of their jobs and responsibilities:

For the purpose of providing support for legal arguments and decisions, researchers perform an analysis of many aspects of the law, including statutes, regulations, and case law.

Documentation: They are responsible for compiling legal research into documents that are well-organized and easy to access. Examples of these materials include legal briefs and research reports.

Legal researchers typically possess a high level of expertise in one or more subfields of the legal profession.

Regulation of Legal Services is Discussed in Chapter 14

The regulation of legal services is absolutely necessary for preserving the honor of the legal profession, safeguarding the interests of clients, and ensuring that legal assistance is offered in a manner that is both ethical and competent. In this chapter, we will discuss the many different facets of legal services regulation, such as the function of bar associations, the standards for licensing and admission, the ethical rules, the disciplinary procedures, and the ever-changing landscape of legal services regulation.

1. An Overview of the Legal Services Regulatory Framework

The regulations that govern the actual practice of law are what are included in the realm of legal services regulation. This rule is absolutely necessary in order to uphold the highest possible ethical standards, guarantee professional competence, and shield clients from attorneys who are unethical or lack the necessary qualifications.

2. The Function of Lawyers' Associations

The regulation of legal services is heavily reliant on the participation of bar associations, such as state and municipal bar associations in the United States. Among their responsibilities are the following:

Licensing and Admission: Bar associations are responsible for establishing the standards that must be met in order to be admitted to the bar. These standards include educational and character requirements. They are in charge of the bar exam, which is a test of candidates' legal knowledge and ability.

Ethical Rules Ethical rules are typically promulgated by bar associations. In the United States, these standards are known as the Model standards of Professional Conduct. The conduct of lawyers is governed by these standards, which include the responsibility of competence, the obligation to maintain confidentiality, and the prohibition against conflicts of interest.

Disciplinary Procedures involve bar associations conducting investigations and hearing appeals regarding complaints against attorneys alleged to have committed ethical infractions. In instances of egregious misbehavior, they have the authority to impose sanctions such as suspension or even disbarment.

Continuing Legal Education (CLE): Many bar associations mandate that attorneys participate in ongoing education in order to keep themselves abreast of recent advancements in the law and to ensure that they remain competent.

3. Prerequisites for Obtaining a License and Admission

The standards for licensing and admittance change depending on the jurisdiction, however they almost always comprise the following components:

Educational Requirements In order to practice law, a person must normally get a Juris Doctor (J.D.) or another law degree that is equivalent from a school that is recognized and approved. It is possible that foreign-educated lawyers will be compelled to provide evidence of their qualifications in certain jurisdictions.

The bar exam is a test of a candidate's knowledge of legal principles as well as their ability to apply those ideas in real-world scenarios. It begins with a written test and then moves on to a performance test or a multistate bar exam (MBE), depending on the circumstances.

Character and Fitness: Applicants are required to demonstrate that they have a high moral character and are physically and mentally capable of practicing law. This requires the submission of character references, background checks, and a review of any previous disciplinary or legal history, if applicable.

Successful completion of the Multistate Professional Responsibility Examination (MPRE) The Multistate Professional Responsibility Examination (MPRE) examines candidates' understanding of professional ethics. It is normally necessary in order to be admitted to the bar.

Oath and Licensing: Applicants are frequently required to take an oath of office and are then licensed to practice law once all of these conditions have been satisfied.

4. Codes of Ethics and the Conduct of a Professional

The regulation of legal services must begin with the establishment of ethical guidelines and standards of professional conduct. The American Bar Association (ABA) Model guidelines of Professional Conduct are used as a foundation for ethical guidelines in many different jurisdictions. These rules were produced by the ABA. The following are fundamental ethical principles:

In order to maintain client confidentiality, attorneys are required to refrain from disclosing any information about their clients unless they have received prior informed consent.

Attorneys are required to offer professional counsel to their clients, which involves keeping abreast of recent developments in the law, zealously representing their clients, and possessing the appropriate skills and knowledge.

In the event that a conflict of interest cannot be avoided, the attorney is obligated to either get the informed consent of all clients who could be impacted or to withdraw from representing those clients.

Representation with Zeal It is expected of attorneys to represent their clients' interests with as much zeal as possible within the parameters of the law.

Integrity and frankness: When communicating with their clients, the court, and other parties, attorneys are expected to maintain integrity and directness.

Access to Justice: Lawyers have an ethical obligation to provide free legal services and to encourage access to justice for populations that are not adequately serviced by the legal system.

5. Procedures Regarding Discipline

When attorneys break the standards of professional behavior, disciplinary actions are taken against them to rectify their misconduct. The following are some of the possible procedures:

Complaints and Investigations: Disciplinary authorities receive complaints from clients or other parties. These complaints can lead to an investigation. Investigations are carried out in order to determine whether or not the allegations have any basis in fact.

Resolutions in an Informal Setting: Some disciplinary issues may be able to be resolved in an informal setting, such as by issuing admonitions or providing counseling for minor offenses.

Formal Proceedings: The more serious cases are taken through the formal proceedings of the disciplinary system. Hearings, the presenting of evidence, and arguments before a judge could all fall under this category.

Sanctions: If the allegations of misbehavior are found to be true, then sanctions may be applied. The severity of the sanction can vary from a private reprimand to a public censure, suspension, or even disbarment.

Appeals: Legal professionals who are facing disciplinary actions may have the ability to appeal decisions made by lower authorities to a higher one.

6. The Changing Climate of the Regulatory Environment for Legal Services

The environment of legal services is changing, including developments that pose a threat to conventional approaches of regulatory oversight. The following are some important recent developments:

Alternative Legal Service Providers The delivery of legal services is undergoing significant change as a result of the emergence of new models of legal service delivery, such as legal technology companies. As a result, there have been conversations about modifying regulations in order to account for these developments.

Concerns have been expressed concerning the impact that allowing non-lawyers to engage in the ownership and management of law firms could have on both legal ethics and professional accountability, and multidisciplinary practice has been brought up as a possible solution to this problem.

Access to Justice: The legal profession is dealing with ways to boost access to justice for marginalized communities, including examining creative regulatory techniques and non-lawyer legal practitioners. One of the ways that they are considering is expanding the number of legal practitioners who are not lawyers.

The use of technology in legal practice, such as artificial intelligence and online legal platforms, poses ethical and regulatory difficulties pertaining to confidentiality, competence, and the unauthorized practice of law. These challenges are brought about by the intersection of technology and the legal profession.

7. Regulations Concerning International Legal Services

The regulation of legal services differs greatly from country to country due to the fact that each country has its own distinct legal system, customs, and regulatory institutions. The following are important international considerations:

The acceptance of legal credentials and bar admissions across international borders is a difficult subject that requires agreements and the harmonization of norms. One way to address this issue is through mutual recognition.

Harmonization of Ethical norms The goal of efforts to harmonize ethical norms for attorneys on a worldwide scale is to make it easier for lawyers around the world to practice law while still upholding ethical standards.

Practice Across Borders The expansion of globalization has led to an increase in the practice of law across borders, which has necessitated the establishment of clear regulations for attorneys who operate in several jurisdictions.

8. Developments in the Regulatory Framework for Legal Services

As a response to the shifting nature of the legal landscape, regulatory authorities are investigating novel approaches to regulation, such as the following:

Sandbox regulation: In some countries, regulatory sandboxes have been built in order to permit the controlled testing of innovative models and technology for the delivery of legal services.

Regulatory Reform: In order to accommodate new practice models while still preserving ethical standards, regulators are currently exploring making adjustments to existing laws and criteria.

Legal Practitioners Who Are Not Lawyers In order to expand people's access to justice, certain jurisdictions are contemplating whether or not to license and regulate legal practitioners who are not lawyers.

9. Obstacles Facing the Supervision of Legal Services

The regulation of legal services is confronted with a number of issues, including the following:

Because the regulation of legal services is both complicated and considerably different from one jurisdiction to another, it is difficult for attorneys to work in multiple countries at the same time.

Access to Justice: Ensuring that underserved communities have access to justice is a huge concern, and debates are still going on about the best way to strike a balance between more regulatory protections and greater access.

Technology's Rapid Advancement The rapid advancement of legal technology raises ethical and regulatory issues, including worries about data privacy and cybersecurity. These challenges are brought about by the quick advancement of legal technology.

Perception in the Public Eye: It is a continual struggle to preserve the public's trust in the legal profession and the regulatory system, which is especially difficult to do in the face of high-profile legal misconduct cases.

Practicing for Tests is Covered in Chapter 15

When it comes to effective exam preparation for any test, including the Multistate Professional Responsibility Examination (MPRE), practice tests are an essential component. In this chapter, we will discuss the significance of practice tests, walk you through some effective methods for completing them, and provide pointers on how to get the most out of your time spent studying so that you can do well on the MPRE. Whether you are a law student or an attorney in active practice, taking practice examinations with a method that is well-structured can considerably improve both your self-assurance and your performance.

1. The Importance of Practicing for Actual Tests

There are a number of reasons why practice examinations are such essential tools:

Familiarity with the Test Format: Practice examinations are designed to replicate the organization and layout of the real MPRE. If you are familiar with the test arrangement, it will be easier for you to efficiently manage your time.

The MPRE is comprised of different types of questions, the most common of which are multiple-choice inquiries of varied degrees of difficulty. You'll be able to adjust to these different kinds of questions with consistent practice.

Knowledge Application Taking practice tests gives you the chance to put your understanding of professional ethics and the Model Rules of Professional Conduct to use in real-world situations.

Identifying Weaknesses: Regular practice is the best way to uncover areas of your knowledge or skill set in which you may be lacking or where you may have gaps. This permits studies to be more narrowly focused.

Test-Taking methods: Practicing under timed conditions enables you to establish test-taking methods for managing time, eliminating wrong answer choices, and picking the most appropriate response.

2. Formulating a Game Plan for Your Mock Exams

In order to effectively prepare for a practice exam, you will need a plan that is well-structured. The following is a guide to getting started:

Evaluation: The evaluation should start with a diagnostic evaluation. You should begin by evaluating your starting point by taking a preliminary practice exam without significant prior preparation.

Choose Reliable Study tools Pick credible study tools, such as official MPRE practice examinations, review courses, or study manuals that are available for purchase.

Making a Study calendar: Make sure to include enough time in your study calendar to complete any necessary practice tests. Think about how much time you have available to study overall, as well as how many practice tests you can actually expect to pass.

Keeping Tabs on Your Advancement Create a system to keep tabs on your advancement, such as a study notebook or digital tools, and do it often. Keep track of your results, the areas that gave you the most trouble, and how much you've improved over time.

3. Methods of Preparatory Work

Follow an organized strategy to your practice exams in order to get the most out of them:

Conditions Timed: Recreate the atmosphere of the real test by staying within the allotted amount of time. The Multiple-Part Question Examination (MPRE) consists of sixty questions that must be answered within two hours, with approximately two minutes allotted to each question.

Randomized Practice In order to imitate the wide variety of questions that will be found on the MPRE, you should randomize the themes and question types that appear on your practice examinations.

Review and Analysis: After completing each of the practice exams, you should go back over your answers and the reasons for them. Examine any errors you may have made and think about why you may have answered a question wrong.

Repeat Weak Areas: If there are particular subject areas or sorts of questions that you struggle with time and time again, you should devote more study time to those specific areas.

Recognize Patterns: When reviewing your past errors, pay attention to any recurring themes. If there are certain types of questions or subjects that you find particularly difficult, you should concentrate your studying efforts there.

4. Timing and tempo of the event

Time management is an extremely important skill to have during the MPRE. The following are some suggestions that will assist you in better managing your time:

Maintaining Consistency: When taking practice exams, be sure to regularly time oneself. Make sure that you spend the same amount of time on each question by timing yourself with a stopwatch or a timer.

Initial Skimming: To start, you should skim all of the questions in order to gain a sense of the level of difficulty they present. Take note of any questions that appear to be particularly difficult.

If you come across a question that seems too difficult for you to answer right away, consider marking it so that you may come back to it later. Because of this, you won't have to devote too much of your time to tackling a single difficult topic.

When you come across a question that you don't know the answer to, make an educated guess and then go on to the next one. Make a note of the question to return to it if there is time left over at the conclusion of the test.

The first thing you should do is concentrate on the questions that are easy so that you may gain confidence and score more points. Following that, go on to the more difficult ones.

5. A Recap and an Evaluation

The phase in which you assess and analyze your performance after an exam is extremely important to your overall improvement. The following is one way to tackle it:

Immediate check: As soon as you have completed a practice exam, immediately check your answers so that you can continue to keep the questions in your mind while you think about the answers.

Analyze the reasoning behind why you choose the erroneous answer for each question and then answer the question. Were you unable to answer correctly because of a lack of information, a misunderstanding of the question, or any other factor?

Keep a Log of Your Errors One thing you should do is keep a log of the different kinds of errors you make. This assists you in recognizing patterns as well as places that could want some work.

After you have analyzed your errors, you should then return to your study materials or resources in order to strengthen your knowledge in the areas that you have identified as needing improvement.

You might consider retaking practice exams, particularly those on which you fared poorly, when you have had sufficient time to review and understand the material.

6. Exam Conditions That Were Modeled

As you move through your preparation for the MPRE, it is essential to simulate test settings during your practice exams to the greatest extent possible:

Environments That Are Quiet You should take your practice examinations in environments that are as quiet as possible and free of any potential distractions.

When taking practice exams, it is important to imitate the conditions of the actual exam as closely as possible; therefore, you should not use any notes, reference materials, or other outside sources.

Technology and Equipment: When you are practicing for the exam, utilize the same equipment, such as a computer or pencil, that you would use during the actual test.

You should get into the habit of simulating the optional break on the MPRE by simulating it during your practice examinations by taking brief breaks or eating snacks.

7. Keeping Tabs on Your Advancement and Establishing Objectives

It is absolutely necessary to keep tabs on your advancement in order to establish clear objectives and standards:

Improve your score by keeping track of how you perform on your practice exams over time. Your objective should be to maintain a steady improvement in how well you perform.

Defining Your Objectives: Before beginning your practice tests, define your objectives in detail. For each test, you could set a goal such as getting a specific percentage of the questions right or completing the whole thing within the time limit.

Using the results of your practice exams to direct your study efforts is an example of targeted study. Focus your attention on the areas that continue to display shortcomings.

Expectations That Are Accurate Determine your starting place and the amount of time you have available to prepare for the MPRE, and then set goals that are accurate but yet challenging.

Using the Official MPRE Practice Exams as a Study Tool

Official MPRE practice tests, which are made available by the National Conference of Bar Examiners (NCBE), are extremely helpful resources for the following reasons:

Authenticity: When it comes to the question format and content, the official practice examinations are going to be the most similar to the actual MPRE that you can acquire.

Official Explanations: The NCBE provides official explanations for each question, which might assist you in comprehending the logic behind the answers that are considered right.

Experience That Is Simulated Completing authentic practice examinations can assist you in becoming accustomed to the specific qualities that are found in MPRE questions.

Scoring and Interpretation: The official practice tests come with extensive scoring and interpretations, which might be of assistance to you during the process of reviewing.

9. Striking a Balance Between the Use of Practice Exams and Study Materials

Even though practice examinations are extremely important, you still need to factor them into your entire study strategy:

Combine Practice and Study: In order to solidify your comprehension of ethical norms, you should combine the experience you gain from practicing with the knowledge you gain from studying materials such as textbooks, study guides, and courses.

Practice According to an arrange: Make sure to arrange some mock exams for yourself. To ensure that you are consistently practicing, you should select certain days or times for the practice exams.

study on a Regular Basis: You should make sure that you schedule enough time in your schedule to regularly study and analyze your practice tests.

10. Methods for Overcoming Test Anxiety

The fear of performing poorly on a test is quite frequent, however there are ways to combat it:

Techniques Relating to BreathingIn order to lessen feelings of worry and improve concentration, try practicing deep breathing exercises.

Replace negative ideas with positive affirmations, and bring to mind that you are well-prepared and capable. Positive self-talk.

Visualization is a great tool for boosting confidence since you may imagine yourself passing the test and having positive results.

Physical Health: Make it a priority to maintain a healthy lifestyle by getting sufficient amounts of sleep, regularly engaging in physical activity, and eating a well-balanced diet.

11. The Last Few Days Prior to the Examination

As the day of the MPRE exam draws closer, here are some tips to help you make the most of your remaining time studying:

Exams Serving as Final Practice Focus on targeted review and taking one or two exams serving as final practice in the days coming up to the exam in order to enhance your confidence.

Don't Push It: Resist the urge to cram or overburden yourself with an excessive amount of studying. Strive for relaxation and equilibrium at the same time.

Maintaining a healthy routine, including adhering to a regular sleep schedule, being hydrated, and eating well, will allow for optimal performance on the day of the exam.

Review the logistics of the exam, such as where it will be held, when it will begin, and what forms of identification will be necessary.

12. Strategies for the Day of the Exam

On the day of the MPRE, you should put the following plans into action:

go There Early: Make sure to give yourself enough of time to go to the testing location when you arrive there. The tension level can rise when there are delays.

Maintain your composure and work on relaxing using the techniques provided. Before you start the test, make sure to take a few long, slow breaths.

Take Your Time to Read: It is important to pay great attention to the way queries are posed. It's possible to make a mistake by misreading a question.

Time Management: Be sure to answer each question within the allocated amount of time. Take care not to concentrate on a single query for an excessive amount of time.

If you come across a question that is very difficult for you, mark it as "flagged" and come back to it later if you have the opportunity.

Check for Obvious Errors and Misinterpretations: If you have the time, go back through your responses and check for any obvious errors or misinterpretations.

Utilize Break Time: If you decide to take the break that is provided, use it to revitalize yourself and concentrate your attention on the remaining portion of the test.

13. A Refection Following the Exam

After the MPRE, you should evaluate your performance as follows:

Avoiding tension After the Exam Refraining from discussing the exam with other people, as this could lead to more tension after the exam.

Relaxation: Before the test, plan some activities that will help you unwind and relax so that you can do better.

Feedback and Adaptation: If necessary, adjust your study plan for future preparations based on the insights you gained from the exam.

14. The Opportunity to Start Over

You have the opportunity to retake the test in the event that your performance on the MPRE is not up to par with what was anticipated:

Review both your preparation and performance in order to pinpoint any weak spots that need to be addressed during the assessment.

Modifications to Your Study Plan You should make modifications to your study plan so that it focuses on the precise areas in which you have room for development.

Exam Simulations: Be sure to keep simulating tests as part of your study routine, paying close attention to the areas in which you need improvement.

repeat the Exam with a Clear Strategy If you decide to repeat the exam, you should do so with a specific strategy in mind, drawing from the experience you obtained from your first attempt.

Day of the MPRE Exam, Chapter 16

The day of the test is an important milestone on the path to become a qualified attorney, and it is critical to approach it with preparation, self-assurance, and a clear game plan in order to be successful. In this chapter, we will walk you through everything you need to know about the day of the MPRE test, from the preparations you should make before the test to what you should anticipate happening on the day of the exam to the post-test activities and tactics you should implement. You will emerge from this chapter with the knowledge and skills necessary to tackle the MPRE with confidence and increase the likelihood of your passing it.

1. Studying for the Tests Beforehand

Before the day of the MPRE test arrives, there are a few crucial preparations that must be completed in order to ensure that you are up to the challenge:

Verify That You Are Registered: Be certain that you have received confirmation of your registration for the MPRE, and double check the date and place of your examination.

Identification: Ensure that you are in possession of a legitimate photo identification card issued by the government, such as a driver's license or a passport. This is going to be required in order to check in at the testing center.

Ticket to Take the Exam You will need to bring your MPRE admittance ticket, which can be accessed through your NCBE account.

Prepare the necessary materials for the test, which include pencils with a number 2 on them, erasers, a highlighter, and a timepiece that is an analog watch but does not have an audible alarm.

Timing Your Practice Exams You should continue to practice under timed situations in order to enhance your skills in time management.

Rest and Nutrition: In the days preceding up to the exam, make getting enough sleep and eating a healthy, well-rounded diet your top priorities. Your mental performance can be considerably influenced by factors such as how well you eat and sleep.

Visit the Test Center You should become familiar with the location of the test center as well as any specific directions or requirements that have been provided by the NCBE.

Plan B: Think about how you will get to the testing facility, and make sure you have a backup plan in case there are any unforeseen complications or holdups.

2. The Evening Before the MMPIA Exam

The night before the MPRE is an important time for both last-minute preparations and unwinding before the test. The following is what you ought to be concentrating on:

Review of the Checklist: Look over your checklist of things that need to be done to make sure you haven't forgotten anything.

Dinner and Hydration: Make sure you have a healthy dinner and drink plenty of water. For the sake of your stomach, stay away from foods that are particularly heavy, hot, or foreign.

Relaxation: In order to calm your anxiety, try engaging in some relaxation practices such as deep breathing or meditation.

Prepare Your daily Routine It is important to prepare your daily routine the night before. This involves choosing what to wear, setting an alarm, and arranging your things in an organized manner.

In order to ensure that you are well-rested and aware on the day of the test, you should strive to get a quality night's sleep.

3. The Format and Structure of the MPRE Exam

It is crucial to have a solid understanding of the format and structure of the MPRE in order to approach the test day with confidence. There are two parts to the MPRE, which are as follows:

Questions on Ethics: The first section of this exam consists of a total of sixty multiple-choice questions that cover a wide range of subjects including professional responsibility, ethics, and the Model Rules of Professional Conduct. These questions are asked during the session that takes place in the morning.

Unscored Questions: During the afternoon session, you will come across six questions that will not be scored. These questions are randomly distributed throughout the test and are utilized for the development of future examinations.

Scoring: The 60 scored questions are the only ones that count toward your score on the MPRE; the other questions, which were not scored, have no bearing on it at all.

Time Management: You will have two hours to answer all 60 scored questions, which comes out to about two minutes for each question on average.

4. Check-In at the MPRE Examination Center

Get to the testing facility in plenty of time to spare before it closes. The following are the steps that are included in the check-in process:

Identification: Along with your admission ticket, you are required to present a photo ID that was issued by the government for verification purposes.

The materials for the test will be handed out to you at this time. These resources may include answer sheets and scratch paper. Make sure that you have access to all of the materials that you require.

Security Measures You should be prepared for security measures, which may include bag checks, metal detectors, and other scanning procedures. Help speed up the process by working together with the personnel at the testing center.

Rules for the Testing Center It is important that you get familiar with the rules and regulations of the testing center, particularly the standards governing acceptable behavior, breaks, and electronic devices.

5. Techniques for Overcoming Test Anxiety

Anxiety before a test is very normal and can adversely effect your performance. On the day of the MPRE, the following are some techniques to help reduce anxiety:

Exercises in Deep Breathing Perform exercises in deep breathing in order to relax and lessen anxiety both before and while taking the test.

Replace negative ideas with positive affirmations, and bring to mind that you are well-prepared and capable. Positive self-talk.

Visualization is a great way to build your confidence since you may imagine yourself performing well on the test and having positive results.

Physical Health: Make it a priority to maintain a healthy lifestyle by getting sufficient amounts of sleep, regularly engaging in physical activity, and eating a well-balanced diet.

6. Tactics to Implement During the MPRE

Utilize the following techniques while taking the MPRE in order to improve your overall performance:

Paying Close Attention To: Carefully read each question and make sure that you have a complete comprehension of both the substance and the context.

Time management requires that you answer each question within the allocated amount of time, which is approximately two minutes. If you find yourself unable to answer a question, it is best to hazard an educated guess and move on to the next one before you run out of time.

If you come across a question that is extremely difficult to answer, you should mark it as problematic and then go on to the next one. You are free to return to questions that you have flagged at a later time if you have the opportunity.

Process of Elimination: When there are plainly erroneous answer alternatives, use the process of elimination to narrow down your options. This will reduce the number of choices available to you, which will ultimately improve your odds of selecting the appropriate response.

Since there is no penalty for making educated guesses on the MPRE, it is imperative that you submit an answer for each and every question, even if you are unsure of the correct response.

Review Your Answers Before Submitting: If you have the time, go back over your responses and make sure there aren't any glaring errors or misunderstandings.

Do not engage in excessive mental deliberation or second-guessing of your decisions. Put your faith in both your experience and your instincts.

7. Taking Advantage of Breaks

The morning and afternoon sections of the MPRE are separated by a break that is entirely voluntary. Here is how you may make the most of this break:

Bring some snacks and drink with you so that you can keep yourself energized and hydrated while you're taking your break.

Stretch Your Legs and Walk Around: If you want to revitalize your body and mind, take this time to stretch your legs and walk around.

Avoid Engaging in unpleasant talks: During the break, you should try to avoid engaging in unpleasant talks or discussing the morning's session. Put your attention on unwinding.

Make sure that you get back to your testing station in plenty of time so that you can get the afternoon session started.

8. Contemplation of the Test Results

Engage in post-test reflection once you have finished the MPRE by thinking about the following:

Avoiding Stress After the Test Refraining from Discussing the Exam with Others Refraining from discussing the exam with others may raise stress after the test.

Activities for Relaxation: After the test, schedule some activities for relaxation so that you may decompress and reduce your stress.

Feedback and Adaptation: If necessary, adjust your study plan for future preparations based on the insights you gained from the exam.

39. The Ratings and the Outcomes

On the MPRE, your score is based on a scale that ranges from 50 to 150, and the passing score is commonly considered to be 85. Your results will typically be made accessible to you within a period of five weeks after the date of the test. Sign in to your NCBE account so that you may access your scores.

Review of Your Score: If you are concerned about your score, you have the option to ask for a review of your score for an extra charge. During the evaluation, we will determine whether or not your comments were graded appropriately.

10. The Opportunity to Start Over

You have the opportunity to retake the test in the event that your performance on the MPRE is not up to par with what was anticipated:

Review both your preparation and performance in order to pinpoint any weak spots that need to be addressed during the assessment.

Modifications to Your Study Plan You should make modifications to your study plan so that it focuses on the precise areas in which you have room for development.

Exam Simulations: Be sure to keep simulating tests as part of your study routine, paying close attention to the areas in which you need improvement.

repeat the Exam with a Clear Strategy If you decide to repeat the exam, you should do so with a specific strategy in mind, drawing from the experience you obtained from your first attempt.

11. Some Closing Considerations and Congratulations

Congratulations on achieving your goal of finishing the MPRE and taking a major step forward in your legal career! It is important to keep in mind that the Multistate Professional Responsibility Exam (MPRE) is just one step on the path to becoming a fully qualified attorney. This is true regardless of whether or not you pass the exam. Make the most of your experiences to improve your level of preparation and tackle future problems with self-assurance. Legal ethics and professional responsibility are fundamental components of the legal profession; therefore, the time and effort you devote to become an expert in these areas will pay off in the long run for you professionally.

After the Examination: Chapter 17

After you have finished the Multistate Professional Responsibility Examination (MPRE), it is time to transfer your focus from test preparation to post-exam activities and considerations. This is an important step in the process of becoming licensed in several states. This chapter will walk you through what to do after the exam, including what to do while you wait for your results, how to analyze your score reports, and how to plan your next actions, regardless of whether you passed the MPRE the first time or not.

1. Awaiting the Results of the MPRE

After you have finished the MPRE, the first thing you will need to do is wait for the results. The MPRE scores are normally made available by the National Conference of Bar Examiners (NCBE) within five weeks of the date of the examination. It is important to remember to practice patience throughout this waiting period and to keep your attention focused on the plans you have for after the exam.

2. While You Are Waiting, What Can You Do?

You can put your time to good use while you are waiting for the results of your MPRE by doing the following:

Take a break from your rigorous studying to give yourself some downtime and give yourself permission to unwind and de-stress. Take part in pursuits that will assist you in unwinding and relieving stress.

Consider Your Experience on the MPRE as You Evaluate Your PerformanceThink about your performance on the MPRE. Where did you succeed, and where did you run into difficulties? Make use of this reflection to guide your future study methods and techniques for approaching tests.

Review your post-test reflection as well as any notes or records you kept while you were studying, and then go to the next step of the post-test analysis. Take note of any areas in which you experienced a predominance of either strength or weakness.

Prepare for the Next Steps: Depending on the outcomes of the test, you may need to prepare for the steps that come after this one. Think about if you want to further your education in the law, study for the bar exam, or take any other steps that are linked to your career.

3. Being Familiar with the MPRE Score Reports

You will be sent a score report from the NCBE once your MPRE results are available to be seen. It is essential to have a solid understanding of the following aspects of the score report:

Score on a Scale: The MPRE has a scaled score that ranges from 50 to 150. The scaled score that you received will decide whether or not you passed the test.

Score Required to Pass: The minimum score required to pass the MPRE is different in each jurisdiction. The minimum required score to pass an exam is often about 85, but this number can differ depending on the jurisdiction.

Score in Its Raw Form: Your score in its raw form is based on the number of questions that you answered correctly. The procedure of statistical equating is used to convert the raw score into a scaled score from the raw score.

Your performance is compared to that of other people who took the MPRE during the same administration that you did, and your percentile rank indicates how you fared in that comparison. For instance, if you scored higher than 75 percent of the people who took the test, it indicates that you are in the 75th percentile.

4. Analyzing Your Performance on the MPRE

Your score on the MPRE can be interpreted in one of two ways, depending on whether or not you passed the exam:

You have successfully passed the MPRE if the scaled score you received on the exam is equal to or higher than the score that was designated as the passing score in your jurisdiction. Many congratulations to you! Your score on the MPRE can now be used for your application to join the bar or for any other purpose required by your jurisdiction.

Your performance on the MPRE was not satisfactory if your scaled score was lower than the minimum required to pass the exam. Do not allow yourself to become disheartened; the majority of test-takers fail the exam on their very first attempt. Instead, make use of your score report as a diagnostic instrument to discover problem areas that need for additional study.

5. Making Choices Regarding Your Future Actions

Your next steps will be determined by your score on the MPRE as well as by your long-term professional goals:

If You Are Successful:

Honor your accomplishments and successes by throwing a party.

Review the precise conditions that must be met in your state or province in order to use your MPRE score in your application to the bar.

Either further your study in the law or move on to the next level of your professional career.

If You Are a Failure:

Examine the breakdown of your scores to determine the components in which you performed the least well.

Consider your approach to studying and think about any changes you could make to it to get better results the next time you take the test.

Determine when you wish to retake the MPRE while taking into consideration the eligibility conditions of your jurisdiction.

6. Getting Ready to Take the Exam Again

It is imperative that you gather your thoughts and make plans to retake the MPRE if you were not successful the first time. A strategic strategy that can help you boost your chances of success is as follows:

Analyzing the Score Report In this step, you will examine your score report in great detail in order to pinpoint the particular subject matter areas in which you performed poorly. This will play a role in the formation of your study plan.

alterations to Your Study strategy You should make any necessary alterations to your study strategy. Concentrate on the areas in which you fared poorly and devote extra attention to the subjects involved in those areas.

Targeted Practice Incorporate additional practice exams, concentrating specifically on the categories of questions and subject matter that proved challenging for you in the past.

Enhanced Review: Create a comprehensive review process that includes a comprehensive investigation of ethical principles and standards in the areas in which you are the most deficient.

Study materials To further solidify what you've learned, you should really contemplate employing a variety of study materials, such as extra textbooks, study guides, or even online courses.

Maintaining a Regular Study Schedule It is important to maintain a regular study schedule in order to ensure that your preparation is exhaustive and that you continue to progress.

Exam-Taking tactics: Go over your test-taking tactics and make any necessary adjustments. Make sure that you are able to successfully manage your time and that you are familiar with the format of the questions that will be on the MPRE.

Simulation of the Examination Before attempting the retake, you should imitate the conditions of the examination by taking full-length practice tests. You'll find that this helps you acquire confidence as well as adjust to the setting of the test.

7. Taking the MPRE all over again

After you have completed your preparation for the MPRE retake, you will need to sign up for the next available exam day in order to take the test again. The following is a guide for how to approach a retake:

Registration: Log in to your NCBE account and use that account to register for the MPRE retake. Check that you are eligible to retake the test in accordance with the regulations of the jurisdiction in which you live.

Create a fresh study plan that takes into account the things you've learnt from your last effort and use those to guide your current approach. Concentrate on improving your performance in areas where you struggle while you continue to hone your skills in areas where you excel.

Taking Additional Practice examinations: Taking additional practice examinations is a great way to continue honing your test-taking abilities and expanding your knowledge of ethical principles.

Time Management: Make time management a top priority during your retake to ensure that you are able to finish all of the questions within the allotted amount of time.

Implement the test-day methods you've devised during your preparations so that you can achieve the best possible results. Keep your cool, refrain from overthinking, and have faith in what you already know.

8. Using the Score You Received on the MPRE

After you have successfully completed the MPRE, you have many options for how to put your score to use:

Score on the Multistate Professional Responsibility Examination (MPREE) is typically required for admission to the bar. If you want to know how to send in your MPRE score as part of the application procedure, you should look into the requirements that apply to your particular country.

Transfer of Scores: If you want to practice law in more than one jurisdiction, you may be required to transfer your score on the Multistate Professional

Responsibility Examination (MPRE) to each jurisdiction. In order to facilitate this process, the NCBE provides a Score Services Portal.

Be aware that your MPRE results will normally only be valid for a set period of time, typically ranging between two and three years depending on the jurisdiction in which you will be using them. When applying for admission to the bar, you need to make sure that your score is still valid.

9. Recognizing and Honoring Your Success

It is a notable accomplishment that displays your dedication to maintaining ethical standards in the legal profession to have passed the Multistate Professional Responsibility Exam (MPRE). Honor your accomplishments, and let them serve as inspiration for you as you move on in your legal career.

10. Post-Exam Introspection and Personal Development

After taking the MPRE, it is important to think back on your experience and use it as a springboard for personal development, regardless of whether you passed or failed the exam.

Take a Look Back at Your Trip: Consider your journey through the MPRE, beginning with the preparations you made initially and ending with the score report you received. Gain an understanding of what went well and what aspects could use some work.

Make the most of this learning opportunity by applying what you've learned from your MPRE experience to future endeavors. Think about how it has helped you develop both personally and professionally throughout the years.

You should use the ethical ideas and rules that you've learnt while studying for the MPRE as the basis for your legal profession and incorporate them into your practice. It is necessary to uphold these principles in order to develop trust within the legal profession and to safeguard the integrity of the legal system.

Plans for the Future: Make plans for your future pursuits in the legal sector, such as applying for admission to the bar and studying or working in the subfields of law that match with your professional aspirations and areas of interest.

Practice Questions and Answers Explanations 2023-2024

Question 1
Which of the following statements accurately describes the attorney-client privilege under the Model Rules of Professional Conduct?

A) The privilege covers all communications between a client and their attorney, including those made in the presence of third parties.
B) The privilege applies even after the death of the client.
C) The privilege is limited to confidential communications made for the purpose of obtaining legal advice.
D) The privilege cannot be waived by the client.

Answer 1: C
Explanation: The attorney-client privilege, as per the Model Rules, is limited to confidential communications made for the purpose of obtaining legal advice. Options A, B, and D contain inaccurate statements.

Question 2
An attorney has discovered that a document in their possession was inadvertently sent to them by opposing counsel. The attorney knows that the document contains confidential information of the opposing party. What is the attorney's ethical duty in this situation?

A) The attorney must promptly return the document without examining its contents.
B) The attorney may keep the document and use the confidential information to their advantage.
C) The attorney must notify opposing counsel and return the document without using or disclosing the confidential information.
D) The attorney should wait for the opposing party to request the return of the document.

Answer 2: C
Explanation: The attorney's ethical duty is to promptly notify opposing counsel and return the document without using or disclosing the confidential information. This is in line with the duty to protect the attorney-client privilege and maintain professional integrity.

Question 3

Under the Model Rules of Professional Conduct, an attorney's conflict of interest may be imputed to another attorney in the same firm if:

A) The conflict arises from a personal interest unrelated to the firm's business.
B) The other attorney is a recent law school graduate and not yet admitted to the bar.
C) The conflicted attorney is not actively involved in the matter.
D) The clients involved provide informed consent in writing.

Answer 3: C

Explanation: An attorney's conflict of interest may be imputed to another attorney in the same firm if the conflicted attorney is not actively involved in the matter. Option C reflects the imputation rule, while the other options do not accurately represent this concept.

Question 4

Attorney Alice is representing a client in a civil lawsuit against Company X. Subsequently, Alice's law firm is retained by Company X to handle an unrelated contract matter. Under the Model Rules, what is Alice's ethical obligation?

A) Alice must withdraw from representing her client in the civil lawsuit.
B) Alice may continue to represent her client in the civil lawsuit but must withdraw from the unrelated contract matter.
C) Alice may continue to represent her client in the civil lawsuit and the unrelated contract matter without any restrictions.
D) Alice may continue to represent her client in the civil lawsuit but should disclose the representation of Company X in the unrelated matter to her client.

Answer 4: B

Explanation: Under the Model Rules, Attorney Alice must withdraw from the unrelated contract matter involving Company X but may continue representing her client in the civil lawsuit. Option B reflects the appropriate ethical response.

Question 5

Attorney David is preparing to present a witness at a deposition. The opposing counsel requests that David not provide any documents to the witness before the deposition, arguing that this will help ensure the witness's testimony is not influenced by outside materials. What should David do under the Model Rules?

A) David must comply with the opposing counsel's request and not provide any documents to the witness.
B) David may provide documents to the witness if they are relevant to the deposition but should not attempt to unduly influence the witness's testimony.
C) David is required to provide all relevant documents to the witness to ensure they are well-prepared for the deposition.
D) David should request that the opposing counsel provide documents to their witness as well.

Answer 5: B
Explanation: Under the Model Rules, Attorney David may provide documents to the witness if they are relevant to the deposition but should not attempt to unduly influence the witness's testimony. Option B reflects the appropriate ethical approach to this situation.

Question 6

Attorney Emily is representing a client in a criminal case. During the trial, Emily becomes aware that the client intends to commit perjury by providing false testimony on the witness stand. What is Emily's ethical duty in this situation according to the Model Rules of Professional Conduct?

A) Emily must advise the client not to commit perjury and, if necessary, seek permission to withdraw from the representation.
B) Emily should not take any action, as it is the client's decision whether to commit perjury.
C) Emily may assist the client in committing perjury as long as the client is not the first to testify falsely.
D) Emily should immediately disclose the client's intention to commit perjury to the court.

Answer 6: A

Explanation: Attorney Emily's ethical duty, as per the Model Rules, is to advise the client not to commit perjury and, if necessary, seek permission to withdraw from the representation. Option A reflects the appropriate ethical response.

Question 7

Under the Model Rules of Professional Conduct, when can an attorney reveal a client's confidential information without the client's informed consent?

A) If the attorney believes it is necessary to prevent a crime or fraud that is likely to result in death or substantial bodily harm.
B) If the attorney believes it is necessary to protect the attorney's own interests in a legal dispute with the client.
C) If the attorney believes it is necessary to defend the attorney against a malpractice claim.
D) If the attorney believes it is necessary to share the information with colleagues within the law firm.

Answer 7: A
Explanation: Under the Model Rules, an attorney may reveal a client's confidential information without the client's informed consent if the attorney believes it is necessary to prevent a crime or fraud that is likely to result in death or substantial bodily harm. Option A reflects the exception to the duty of confidentiality.

Question 8

Which of the following statements accurately reflects the Model Rules of Professional Conduct regarding an attorney's duties when representing multiple clients?

A) An attorney must prioritize the interests of the client who is paying the highest fee.
B) An attorney must avoid representing clients with conflicting interests unless each client provides informed consent.
C) An attorney must represent all clients in the same matter regardless of any conflicts of interest.
D) An attorney may represent clients with conflicting interests without obtaining informed consent as long as the attorney believes it is in their best interests.

Answer 8: B

Explanation: According to the Model Rules, an attorney must avoid representing clients with conflicting interests unless each client provides informed consent. Option B accurately reflects the ethical standard for multiple client representation.

Question 9

Attorney Frank has discovered a substantial error in a document submitted to the court by opposing counsel. The error is advantageous to Frank's client. Under the Model Rules of Professional Conduct, what should Frank do?

A) Frank should do nothing and allow the court to discover the error on its own.
B) Frank may use the error to his client's advantage and keep it confidential.
C) Frank is required to disclose the error to the court and opposing counsel.
D) Frank should advise opposing counsel of the error and seek their permission to correct it.

Answer 9: C
Explanation: Under the Model Rules, Attorney Frank is required to disclose the error to the court and opposing counsel. This reflects the duty of candor to the tribunal and professional integrity.

Question 10

In a criminal trial, Attorney Gina is representing the defendant. The defendant intends to testify falsely in their own defense. Under the Model Rules of Professional Conduct, what should Gina do in this situation?

A) Gina must advise the defendant not to testify falsely and seek permission to withdraw from the representation if necessary.
B) Gina should not take any action, as it is the defendant's decision whether to testify falsely.
C) Gina may assist the defendant in testifying falsely as long as the defendant believes it is necessary for their defense.
D) Gina should immediately disclose the defendant's intention to testify falsely to the court.

Answer 10: A
Explanation: Attorney Gina's ethical duty, according to the Model Rules, is to advise the defendant not to testify falsely and, if necessary, seek permission to

withdraw from the representation. Option A reflects the appropriate ethical response.

Question 11

Under the Model Rules of Professional Conduct, what is the attorney's duty when they receive a document that they know was inadvertently sent to them by opposing counsel, and the document contains confidential information of the opposing party?

A) The attorney must return the document without reading it.
B) The attorney may keep the document and use the confidential information if it benefits their client.
C) The attorney must notify opposing counsel and return the document without using or disclosing the confidential information.
D) The attorney should wait for opposing counsel to request the return of the document.

Answer 11: C
Explanation: The attorney's duty, according to the Model Rules, is to promptly notify opposing counsel and return the document without using or disclosing the confidential information. This upholds the duty to protect attorney-client privilege and professional ethics.

Question 12

Attorney Henry is representing a client in a civil case against Company Y. Subsequently, Henry's law firm is retained by Company Y for an unrelated contract matter. According to the Model Rules of Professional Conduct, what should Henry do?

A) Henry must withdraw from representing his client in the civil case.
B) Henry may continue to represent his client in the civil case but must withdraw from the unrelated contract matter.
C) Henry may continue to represent his client in the civil case and the unrelated contract matter without any restrictions.
D) Henry may continue to represent his client in the civil case but should disclose the representation of Company Y in the unrelated matter to his client.

Answer 12: B

Explanation: Under the Model Rules, Attorney Henry must withdraw from the unrelated contract matter involving Company Y but may continue representing his client in the civil case. Option B reflects the appropriate ethical response.

Question 13
Attorney Isabelle is aware that her client intends to provide false testimony in a civil trial. Under the Model Rules of Professional Conduct, what is Isabelle's ethical duty?

A) Isabelle must advise the client not to provide false testimony and seek permission to withdraw from the representation if necessary.
B) Isabelle may assist the client in providing false testimony as long as it is relevant to the case.
C) Isabelle should not take any action, as it is the client's decision whether to provide false testimony.
D) Isabelle should immediately disclose the client's intention to provide false testimony to the court.

Answer 13: A
Explanation: According to the Model Rules, Attorney Isabelle's ethical duty is to advise the client not to provide false testimony and seek permission to withdraw from the representation if necessary. Option A reflects the appropriate ethical response.

Question 14
Under the Model Rules of Professional Conduct, when can an attorney reveal a client's confidential information without the client's informed consent?

A) If the attorney believes it is necessary to protect the attorney's own interests in a legal dispute with the client.
B) If the attorney believes it is necessary to defend the attorney against a malpractice claim.
C) If the attorney believes it is necessary to share the information with colleagues within the law firm.
D) If the attorney believes it is necessary to prevent a crime or fraud that is likely to result in death or substantial bodily harm.

Answer 14: D
Explanation: Under the Model Rules, an attorney may reveal a client's confidential information without the client's informed consent if the attorney

believes it is necessary to prevent a crime or fraud that is likely to result in death or substantial bodily harm. Option D reflects the exception to the duty of confidentiality.

Question 15

Which of the following statements accurately reflects the Model Rules of Professional Conduct regarding an attorney's duties when representing multiple clients?

A) An attorney may represent clients with conflicting interests as long as each client provides informed consent.
B) An attorney must prioritize the interests of the client who is paying the highest fee.
C) An attorney must represent all clients in the same matter regardless of any conflicts of interest.
D) An attorney must avoid representing clients with conflicting interests unless each client provides informed consent.

Answer 15: D
Explanation: According to the Model Rules, an attorney must avoid representing clients with conflicting interests unless each client provides informed consent. Option D accurately reflects the ethical standard for multiple client representation.

Question 16

Attorney Jack is aware that a document submitted to the court by opposing counsel contains a substantial error that is advantageous to Jack's client. Under the Model Rules of Professional Conduct, what should Jack do?

A) Jack should do nothing and allow the court to discover the error on its own.
B) Jack may use the error to his client's advantage and keep it confidential.
C) Jack is required to disclose the error to the court and opposing counsel.
D) Jack should advise opposing counsel of the error and seek their permission to correct it.

Answer 16: C
Explanation: Under the Model Rules, Attorney Jack is required to disclose the error to the court and opposing counsel. This reflects the duty of candor to the tribunal and professional integrity.

Question 17

In a criminal trial, Attorney Karen is representing the defendant. The defendant intends to testify falsely in their own defense. Under the Model Rules of Professional Conduct, what should Karen do in this situation?

A) Karen should advise the defendant to testify truthfully, but if the defendant insists on testifying falsely, Karen may assist in presenting the false testimony.
B) Karen should not take any action, as it is the defendant's decision whether to testify falsely.
C) Karen may assist the defendant in testifying falsely as long as it is relevant to the case.
D) Karen must advise the defendant not to testify falsely and seek permission to withdraw from the representation if necessary.

Answer 17: D
Explanation: According to the Model Rules, Attorney Karen's ethical duty is to advise the defendant not to testify falsely and, if necessary, seek permission to withdraw from the representation. Option D reflects the appropriate ethical response.

Question 18

Under the Model Rules of Professional Conduct, an attorney's conflict of interest may be imputed to another attorney in the same firm if:

A) The other attorney is not actively involved in the matter.
B) The conflict arises from a personal interest unrelated to the firm's business.
C) The conflicted attorney is a recent law school graduate and not yet admitted to the bar.
D) The clients involved provide informed consent in writing.

Answer 18: A
Explanation: An attorney's conflict of interest may be imputed to another attorney in the same firm if the conflicted attorney is not actively involved in the matter. Option A reflects the imputation rule, while the other options do not accurately represent this concept.

Question 19

Under the Model Rules of Professional Conduct, when can an attorney reveal a client's confidential information without the client's informed consent?

A) If the attorney believes it is necessary to protect the attorney's own interests in a legal dispute with the client.
B) If the attorney believes it is necessary to share the information with colleagues within the law firm.
C) If the attorney believes it is necessary to prevent a crime or fraud that is likely to result in substantial financial harm.
D) If the attorney believes it is necessary to defend the attorney against a malpractice claim.

Answer 19: C
Explanation: Under the Model Rules, an attorney may reveal a client's confidential information without the client's informed consent if the attorney believes it is necessary to prevent a crime or fraud that is likely to result in substantial financial harm. Option C reflects the exception to the duty of confidentiality.

Question 20

Which of the following statements accurately describes the attorney-client privilege under the Model Rules of Professional Conduct?

A) The privilege is limited to confidential communications made for the purpose of obtaining legal advice.
B) The privilege applies even after the death of the client.
C) The privilege covers all communications between a client and their attorney, including those made in the presence of third parties.
D) The privilege cannot be waived by the client.

Answer 20: A
Explanation: The attorney-client privilege, as per the Model Rules, is limited to confidential communications made for the purpose of obtaining legal advice. Option A accurately represents the attorney-client privilege.

Question 21

Attorney Liam is representing a client in a criminal case. During the trial, Liam becomes aware that the client intends to commit perjury by providing false testimony on the witness stand. What is Liam's ethical duty in this situation according to the Model Rules of Professional Conduct?

A) Liam should advise the client to testify truthfully but may assist in presenting the false testimony if the client insists.
B) Liam should not take any action, as it is the client's decision whether to testify falsely.
C) Liam may assist the client in testifying falsely as long as it is relevant to the case.
D) Liam must advise the client not to commit perjury and, if necessary, seek permission to withdraw from the representation.

Answer 21: D
Explanation: Attorney Liam's ethical duty, according to the Model Rules, is to advise the client not to commit perjury and, if necessary, seek permission to withdraw from the representation. Option D reflects the appropriate ethical response.

Question 22

Under the Model Rules of Professional Conduct, what is the attorney's duty when they receive a document that they know was inadvertently sent to them by opposing counsel, and the document contains confidential information of the opposing party?

A) The attorney must return the document without reading it.
B) The attorney may keep the document and use the confidential information if it benefits their client.
C) The attorney must notify opposing counsel and return the document without using or disclosing the confidential information.
D) The attorney should wait for opposing counsel to request the return of the document.

Answer 22: C
Explanation: The attorney's duty, according to the Model Rules, is to promptly notify opposing counsel and return the document without using or disclosing the confidential information. This upholds the duty to protect attorney-client privilege and professional ethics.

Question 23

Attorney Maria is representing a client in a civil case against Company Z. Subsequently, Maria's law firm is retained by Company Z for an unrelated contract matter. What should Maria do according to the Model Rules of Professional Conduct?

A) Maria must withdraw from representing her client in the civil case.
B) Maria may continue to represent her client in the civil case but must withdraw from the unrelated contract matter.
C) Maria may continue to represent her client in the civil case and the unrelated contract matter without any restrictions.
D) Maria may continue to represent her client in the civil case but should disclose the representation of Company Z in the unrelated matter to her client.

Answer 23: B
Explanation: Under the Model Rules, Attorney Maria must withdraw from the unrelated contract matter involving Company Z but may continue representing her client in the civil case. Option B reflects the appropriate ethical response.

Question 24

Attorney Nathan is aware that his client intends to provide false testimony in a civil trial. Under the Model Rules of Professional Conduct, what is Nathan's ethical duty?

A) Nathan must advise the client not to provide false testimony and seek permission to withdraw from the representation if necessary.
B) Nathan may assist the client in providing false testimony as long as it is relevant to the case.
C) Nathan should not take any action, as it is the client's decision whether to provide false testimony.
D) Nathan should immediately disclose the client's intention to provide false testimony to the court.

Answer 24: A
Explanation: According to the Model Rules, Attorney Nathan's ethical duty is to advise the client not to provide false testimony and, if necessary, seek permission to withdraw from the representation. Option A reflects the appropriate ethical response.

Question 25

Under the Model Rules of Professional Conduct, when can an attorney reveal a client's confidential information without the client's informed consent?

A) If the attorney believes it is necessary to protect the attorney's own interests in a legal dispute with the client.
B) If the attorney believes it is necessary to defend the attorney against a malpractice claim.
C) If the attorney believes it is necessary to share the information with colleagues within the law firm.
D) If the attorney believes it is necessary to prevent a crime or fraud that is likely to result in death or substantial bodily harm.

Answer 25: D
Explanation: Under the Model Rules, an attorney may reveal a client's confidential information without the client's informed consent if the attorney believes it is necessary to prevent a crime or fraud that is likely to result in death or substantial bodily harm. Option D reflects the exception to the duty of confidentiality.

Question 26

Which of the following statements accurately reflects the Model Rules of Professional Conduct regarding an attorney's duties when representing multiple clients?

A) An attorney may represent clients with conflicting interests as long as each client provides informed consent.
B) An attorney must prioritize the interests of the client who is paying the highest fee.
C) An attorney must represent all clients in the same matter regardless of any conflicts of interest.
D) An attorney must avoid representing clients with conflicting interests unless each client provides informed consent.

Answer 26: D
Explanation: According to the Model Rules, an attorney must avoid representing clients with conflicting interests unless each client provides informed consent. Option D accurately reflects the ethical standard for multiple client representation.

Question 27

Attorney Olivia is representing a client in a real estate transaction. The client instructs Olivia to falsify information on the closing documents to reduce the property taxes. What is Olivia's ethical duty according to the Model Rules of Professional Conduct?

A) Olivia may comply with the client's instructions as long as it benefits the client.
B) Olivia must advise the client against falsifying information and should consider withdrawing from the representation if the client insists.
C) Olivia should follow the client's instructions to maintain the attorney-client privilege.
D) Olivia should report the client's instructions to the appropriate taxing authorities.

Answer 27: B
Explanation: Under the Model Rules, Attorney Olivia's ethical duty is to advise the client against falsifying information and consider withdrawing from the representation if the client insists. This upholds ethical standards and professional integrity.

Question 28

Attorney Paul is representing a defendant in a criminal trial. Paul believes the defendant is guilty but is instructed to present a false alibi defense. What should Paul do under the Model Rules of Professional Conduct?

A) Paul may present the false alibi defense if the defendant insists.
B) Paul should present the false alibi defense to provide the defendant with the best possible defense.
C) Paul is required to advise the defendant against presenting a false alibi defense.
D) Paul should immediately report the defendant's intentions to the prosecution.

Answer 28: C
Explanation: According to the Model Rules, Attorney Paul is required to advise the defendant against presenting a false alibi defense. Option C reflects the appropriate ethical response.

Question 29
Under the Model Rules of Professional Conduct, when can an attorney reveal a client's confidential information without the client's informed consent?

A) If the attorney believes it is necessary to protect the attorney's own interests in a legal dispute with the client.
B) If the attorney believes it is necessary to share the information with colleagues within the law firm.
C) If the attorney believes it is necessary to prevent a crime that may result in substantial financial harm.
D) If the attorney believes it is necessary to prevent a crime or fraud that is likely to result in death or substantial bodily harm.

Answer 29: D
Explanation: Under the Model Rules, an attorney may reveal a client's confidential information without the client's informed consent if the attorney believes it is necessary to prevent a crime or fraud that is likely to result in death or substantial bodily harm. Option D reflects the exception to the duty of confidentiality.

Question 30
Which of the following statements accurately describes the attorney-client privilege under the Model Rules of Professional Conduct?

A) The privilege is limited to confidential communications made for the purpose of obtaining legal advice.
B) The privilege applies even after the death of the client.
C) The privilege covers all communications between a client and their attorney, including those made in the presence of third parties.
D) The privilege cannot be waived by the client.

Answer 30: A
Explanation: The attorney-client privilege, as per the Model Rules, is limited to confidential communications made for the purpose of obtaining legal advice. Option A accurately represents the attorney-client privilege.

Question 31

Attorney Quinn is aware that her client intends to provide false testimony in a civil trial. Under the Model Rules of Professional Conduct, what is Quinn's ethical duty?

A) Quinn may assist the client in providing false testimony if it benefits the client.
B) Quinn should not take any action, as it is the client's decision whether to provide false testimony.
C) Quinn must advise the client not to provide false testimony and, if necessary, seek permission to withdraw from the representation.
D) Quinn should immediately disclose the client's intention to provide false testimony to the court.

Answer 31: C
Explanation: According to the Model Rules, Attorney Quinn's ethical duty is to advise the client not to provide false testimony and, if necessary, seek permission to withdraw from the representation. Option C reflects the appropriate ethical response.

Question 32

Attorney Rebecca is representing a client in a personal injury lawsuit. The client intends to exaggerate the extent of their injuries during testimony. What is Rebecca's ethical duty under the Model Rules of Professional Conduct?

A) Rebecca may assist the client in exaggerating their injuries to improve their chances of winning the case.
B) Rebecca should not take any action, as it is the client's decision whether to exaggerate their injuries.
C) Rebecca must advise the client against exaggerating their injuries and, if necessary, seek permission to withdraw from the representation.
D) Rebecca should advise the client to exaggerate their injuries to ensure a favorable outcome.

Answer 32: C
Explanation: Under the Model Rules, Attorney Rebecca's ethical duty is to advise the client against exaggerating their injuries and, if necessary, seek permission to withdraw from the representation. Option C reflects the appropriate ethical response.

Question 33

Under the Model Rules of Professional Conduct, when can an attorney reveal a client's confidential information without the client's informed consent?

A) If the attorney believes it is necessary to protect the attorney's own interests in a legal dispute with the client.
B) If the attorney believes it is necessary to defend the attorney against a malpractice claim.
C) If the attorney believes it is necessary to share the information with colleagues within the law firm.
D) If the attorney believes it is necessary to prevent a crime or fraud that may result in substantial financial harm.

Answer 33: B
Explanation: Under the Model Rules, an attorney may reveal a client's confidential information without the client's informed consent if the attorney believes it is necessary to defend the attorney against a malpractice claim. Option B reflects the exception to the duty of confidentiality.

Question 34

Attorney Sam is representing a client in a criminal case. The client is planning to provide false testimony but has not disclosed this to Sam. What is Sam's ethical duty according to the Model Rules of Professional Conduct?

A) Sam should not take any action and proceed with the representation.
B) Sam must advise the client not to provide false testimony if the issue arises during the trial.
C) Sam should immediately withdraw from the representation to avoid potential ethical violations.
D) Sam should assist the client in providing false testimony to secure a favorable outcome.

Answer 34: B
Explanation: According to the Model Rules, Attorney Sam's ethical duty is to advise the client not to provide false testimony if the issue arises during the trial. Option B reflects the appropriate ethical response.

Question 35

Which of the following statements accurately describes the attorney-client privilege under the Model Rules of Professional Conduct?

A) The privilege applies even after the death of the client.
B) The privilege is limited to confidential communications made for the purpose of obtaining legal advice.
C) The privilege cannot be waived by the client.
D) The privilege covers all communications between a client and their attorney, including those made in the presence of third parties.

Answer 35: B

Explanation: The attorney-client privilege, as per the Model Rules, is limited to confidential communications made for the purpose of obtaining legal advice. Option B accurately represents the attorney-client privilege.

Question 36

Attorney Thomas is aware that his client intends to provide false testimony in a civil trial. Under the Model Rules of Professional Conduct, what is Thomas's ethical duty?

A) Thomas should not take any action, as it is the client's decision whether to provide false testimony.
B) Thomas may assist the client in providing false testimony as long as it is relevant to the case.
C) Thomas must advise the client not to provide false testimony and, if necessary, seek permission to withdraw from the representation.
D) Thomas should immediately disclose the client's intention to provide false testimony to the court.

Answer 36: C

Explanation: According to the Model Rules, Attorney Thomas's ethical duty is to advise the client not to provide false testimony and, if necessary, seek permission to withdraw from the representation. Option C reflects the appropriate ethical response.

Question 37

Under the Model Rules of Professional Conduct, when can an attorney reveal a client's confidential information without the client's informed consent?

A) If the attorney believes it is necessary to protect the attorney's own interests in a legal dispute with the client.
B) If the attorney believes it is necessary to defend the attorney against a malpractice claim.
C) If the attorney believes it is necessary to share the information with colleagues within the law firm.
D) If the attorney believes it is necessary to prevent a crime or fraud that is likely to result in substantial financial harm.

Answer 37: A
Explanation: Under the Model Rules, an attorney may reveal a client's confidential information without the client's informed consent if the attorney believes it is necessary to protect the attorney's own interests in a legal dispute with the client. Option A reflects the exception to the duty of confidentiality.

Question 38

Attorney Ursula is representing a client in a civil matter. During a deposition, Ursula realizes that the opposing counsel is presenting false evidence to the court. What is Ursula's ethical duty under the Model Rules of Professional Conduct?

A) Ursula must advise the opposing counsel to correct the false evidence.
B) Ursula should not take any action, as it is the opposing counsel's responsibility to present evidence.
C) Ursula may use the false evidence to her client's advantage.
D) Ursula must disclose the false evidence to the court and opposing counsel.

Answer 38: D
Explanation: According to the Model Rules, Attorney Ursula's ethical duty is to disclose the false evidence to the court and opposing counsel. Option D reflects the appropriate ethical response.

Question 39

Under the Model Rules of Professional Conduct, what is an attorney's duty if they discover a conflict of interest with a current client?

A) The attorney must promptly disclose the conflict to the client and seek the client's informed consent in writing.
B) The attorney should take no action as long as the conflict does not interfere with their representation.
C) The attorney is required to withdraw from the representation immediately.
D) The attorney may continue representing both clients as long as they believe it is in the best interests of both parties.

Answer 39: A

Explanation: Under the Model Rules, when an attorney discovers a conflict of interest with a current client, the attorney must promptly disclose the conflict to the client and seek the client's informed consent in writing. Option A reflects the appropriate ethical response.

Question 40

Attorney Victor is representing a client in a civil matter. The client instructs Victor to destroy evidence that is unfavorable to the client's case. What is Victor's ethical duty under the Model Rules of Professional Conduct?

A) Victor may comply with the client's instructions to protect the attorney-client privilege.
B) Victor should follow the client's instructions to maintain the attorney-client relationship.
C) Victor is required to advise the client against destroying evidence and consider withdrawing from the representation if the client insists.
D) Victor should seek advice from a colleague within the law firm before taking any action.

Answer 40: C

Explanation: According to the Model Rules, Attorney Victor is required to advise the client against destroying evidence and consider withdrawing from the representation if the client insists. This upholds ethical standards and professional integrity.

Question 41
Under the Model Rules of Professional Conduct, when can an attorney reveal a client's confidential information without the client's informed consent?

A) If the attorney believes it is necessary to prevent a crime or fraud that may result in substantial financial harm.
B) If the attorney believes it is necessary to protect the attorney's own interests in a legal dispute with the client.
C) If the attorney believes it is necessary to share the information with colleagues within the law firm.
D) If the attorney believes it is necessary to prevent a crime or fraud that is likely to result in death or substantial bodily harm.

Answer 41: D
Explanation: Under the Model Rules, an attorney may reveal a client's confidential information without the client's informed consent if the attorney believes it is necessary to prevent a crime or fraud that is likely to result in death or substantial bodily harm. Option D reflects the exception to the duty of confidentiality.

Question 42
Attorney William is representing a client in a civil lawsuit. The client intends to provide false testimony during the trial. What is William's ethical duty under the Model Rules of Professional Conduct?

A) William must advise the client not to provide false testimony and, if necessary, seek permission to withdraw from the representation.
B) William should not take any action, as it is the client's decision whether to provide false testimony.
C) William may assist the client in providing false testimony if it benefits the client.
D) William should immediately disclose the client's intention to provide false testimony to the court.

Answer 42: A
Explanation: According to the Model Rules, Attorney William's ethical duty is to advise the client not to provide false testimony and, if necessary, seek permission to withdraw from the representation. Option A reflects the appropriate ethical response.

Question 43

Under the Model Rules of Professional Conduct, what is the attorney's duty when they receive a document that they know was inadvertently sent to them by opposing counsel, and the document contains confidential information of the opposing party?

A) The attorney must return the document without reading it.
B) The attorney may keep the document and use the confidential information if it benefits their client.
C) The attorney must notify opposing counsel and return the document without using or disclosing the confidential information.
D) The attorney should wait for opposing counsel to request the return of the document.

Answer 43: C
Explanation: The attorney's duty, according to the Model Rules, is to promptly notify opposing counsel and return the document without using or disclosing the confidential information. This upholds the duty to protect attorney-client privilege and professional ethics.

Question 44

Attorney Xavier is representing a client in a personal injury case. The client demands that Xavier disclose the client's confidential settlement offer to the opposing party. What should Xavier do under the Model Rules of Professional Conduct?

A) Xavier may disclose the settlement offer as long as the client insists.
B) Xavier should disclose the settlement offer to maintain a transparent process.
C) Xavier is required to advise the client against disclosing the offer and should consider withdrawing from the representation if the client insists.
D) Xavier should disclose the settlement offer to protect the attorney-client privilege.

Answer 44: C
Explanation: According to the Model Rules, Attorney Xavier is required to advise the client against disclosing the settlement offer and should consider withdrawing from the representation if the client insists. This upholds ethical standards and professional integrity.

Question 45
Under the Model Rules of Professional Conduct, what is the attorney's duty if they discover a conflict of interest with a current client?

A) The attorney should take no action as long as the conflict does not interfere with their representation.
B) The attorney must promptly disclose the conflict to the client and seek the client's informed consent in writing.
C) The attorney is required to withdraw from the representation immediately.
D) The attorney may continue representing both clients as long as they believe it is in the best interests of both parties.

Answer 45: B
Explanation: Under the Model Rules, when an attorney discovers a conflict of interest with a current client, the attorney must promptly disclose the conflict to the client and seek the client's informed consent in writing. Option B reflects the appropriate ethical response.

Question 46
Attorney Yasmine is representing a client in a criminal trial. The client intends to testify falsely in their own defense. What is Yasmine's ethical duty under the Model Rules of Professional Conduct?

A) Yasmine must advise the client to testify truthfully, but if the client insists on testifying falsely, Yasmine may assist in presenting the false testimony.
B) Yasmine should not take any action, as it is the client's decision whether to testify falsely.
C) Yasmine may assist the client in testifying falsely as long as it is relevant to the case.
D) Yasmine must advise the client not to testify falsely and seek permission to withdraw from the representation if necessary.

Answer 46: D
Explanation: According to the Model Rules, Attorney Yasmine's ethical duty is to advise the client not to testify falsely and, if necessary, seek permission to withdraw from the representation. Option D reflects the appropriate ethical response.

Question 47

Under the Model Rules of Professional Conduct, when can an attorney reveal a client's confidential information without the client's informed consent?

A) If the attorney believes it is necessary to protect the attorney's own interests in a legal dispute with the client.
B) If the attorney believes it is necessary to defend the attorney against a malpractice claim.
C) If the attorney believes it is necessary to share the information with colleagues within the law firm.
D) If the attorney believes it is necessary to prevent a crime or fraud that is likely to result in substantial financial harm.

Answer 47: B
Explanation: Under the Model Rules, an attorney may reveal a client's confidential information without the client's informed consent if the attorney believes it is necessary to defend the attorney against a malpractice claim. Option B reflects the exception to the duty of confidentiality.

Question 48

Attorney Zach is representing a client in a civil case. During the trial, Zach becomes aware that the opposing counsel is presenting false evidence to the court. What is Zach's ethical duty under the Model Rules of Professional Conduct?

A) Zach must advise the opposing counsel to correct the false evidence.
B) Zach should not take any action, as it is the opposing counsel's responsibility to present evidence.
C) Zach may use the false evidence to his client's advantage.
D) Zach must disclose the false evidence to the court and opposing counsel.

Answer 48: D
Explanation: According to the Model Rules, Attorney Zach's ethical duty is to disclose the false evidence to the court and opposing counsel. Option D reflects the appropriate ethical response.

Question 49
Under the Model Rules of Professional Conduct, what is the attorney's duty when they discover a conflict of interest with a current client?

A) The attorney should take no action and continue representing both clients.
B) The attorney must promptly disclose the conflict to the client and seek the client's informed consent in writing.
C) The attorney is required to withdraw from the representation immediately.
D) The attorney may continue representing both clients as long as they believe it is in the best interests of both parties.

Answer 49: B
Explanation: Under the Model Rules, when an attorney discovers a conflict of interest with a current client, the attorney must promptly disclose the conflict to the client and seek the client's informed consent in writing. Option B reflects the appropriate ethical response.

Question 50
Attorney Wendy is representing a client in a criminal trial. The client intends to testify falsely in their own defense. Under the Model Rules of Professional Conduct, what should Wendy do in this situation?

A) Wendy must advise the client to testify truthfully, but if the client insists on testifying falsely, Wendy may assist in presenting the false testimony.
B) Wendy should not take any action, as it is the client's decision whether to testify falsely.
C) Wendy may assist the client in testifying falsely as long as it is relevant to the case.
D) Wendy must advise the client not to testify falsely and seek permission to withdraw from the representation if necessary.

Answer 50: D
Explanation: According to the Model Rules, Attorney Wendy's ethical duty is to advise the client not to testify falsely and, if necessary, seek permission to withdraw from the representation. Option D reflects the appropriate ethical response.

Question 51

Under the Model Rules of Professional Conduct, what is an attorney's duty when they discover a conflict of interest with a current client?

A) The attorney should take no action as long as the conflict does not interfere with their representation.
B) The attorney must promptly disclose the conflict to the client and seek the client's informed consent in writing.
C) The attorney is required to withdraw from the representation immediately.
D) The attorney may continue representing both clients as long as they believe it is in the best interests of both parties.

Answer 51: B

Explanation: Under the Model Rules, when an attorney discovers a conflict of interest with a current client, the attorney must promptly disclose the conflict to the client and seek the client's informed consent in writing. Option B reflects the appropriate ethical response.

Question 52

Attorney Xavier is representing a client in a personal injury lawsuit. The client demands that Xavier disclose the client's confidential settlement offer to the opposing party. What should Xavier do under the Model Rules of Professional Conduct?

A) Xavier may disclose the settlement offer as long as the client insists.
B) Xavier should disclose the settlement offer to maintain a transparent process.
C) Xavier is required to advise the client against disclosing the offer and should consider withdrawing from the representation if the client insists.
D) Xavier should disclose the settlement offer to protect the attorney-client privilege.

Answer 52: C

Explanation: According to the Model Rules, Attorney Xavier is required to advise the client against disclosing the settlement offer and should consider withdrawing from the representation if the client insists. This upholds ethical standards and professional integrity.

Question 53

Under the Model Rules of Professional Conduct, when can an attorney reveal a client's confidential information without the client's informed consent?

A) If the attorney believes it is necessary to prevent a crime or fraud that may result in substantial financial harm.
B) If the attorney believes it is necessary to protect the attorney's own interests in a legal dispute with the client.
C) If the attorney believes it is necessary to share the information with colleagues within the law firm.
D) If the attorney believes it is necessary to prevent a crime or fraud that is likely to result in death or substantial bodily harm.

Answer 53: A
Explanation: Under the Model Rules, an attorney may reveal a client's confidential information without the client's informed consent if the attorney believes it is necessary to prevent a crime or fraud that may result in substantial financial harm. Option A reflects the exception to the duty of confidentiality.

Question 54

Attorney William is representing a client in a civil lawsuit. The client intends to provide false testimony during the trial. What is William's ethical duty under the Model Rules of Professional Conduct?

A) William must advise the client not to provide false testimony and, if necessary, seek permission to withdraw from the representation.
B) William should not take any action, as it is the client's decision whether to provide false testimony.
C) William may assist the client in providing false testimony if it benefits the client.
D) William should immediately disclose the client's intention to provide false testimony to the court.

Answer 54: A
Explanation: According to the Model Rules, Attorney William's ethical duty is to advise the client not to provide false testimony and, if necessary, seek permission to withdraw from the representation. Option A reflects the appropriate ethical response.

Question 55

Under the Model Rules of Professional Conduct, what is an attorney's duty when they discover a conflict of interest with a current client?

A) The attorney should take no action and continue representing both clients.
B) The attorney must promptly disclose the conflict to the client and seek the client's informed consent in writing.
C) The attorney is required to withdraw from the representation immediately.
D) The attorney may continue representing both clients as long as they believe it is in the best interests of both parties.

Answer 55: B

Explanation: Under the Model Rules, when an attorney discovers a conflict of interest with a current client, the attorney must promptly disclose the conflict to the client and seek the client's informed consent in writing. Option B reflects the appropriate ethical response.

Question 56

Attorney Yasmine is representing a client in a criminal trial. The client intends to testify falsely in their own defense. What is Yasmine's ethical duty under the Model Rules of Professional Conduct?

A) Yasmine must advise the client to testify truthfully, but if the client insists on testifying falsely, Yasmine may assist in presenting the false testimony.
B) Yasmine should not take any action, as it is the client's decision whether to testify falsely.
C) Yasmine may assist the client in testifying falsely as long as it is relevant to the case.
D) Yasmine must advise the client not to testify falsely and seek permission to withdraw from the representation if necessary.

Answer 56: D

Explanation: According to the Model Rules, Attorney Yasmine's ethical duty is to advise the client not to testify falsely and, if necessary, seek permission to withdraw from the representation. Option D reflects the appropriate ethical response.

Question 57

Under the Model Rules of Professional Conduct, when can an attorney reveal a client's confidential information without the client's informed consent?

A) If the attorney believes it is necessary to protect the attorney's own interests in a legal dispute with the client.
B) If the attorney believes it is necessary to defend the attorney against a malpractice claim.
C) If the attorney believes it is necessary to share the information with colleagues within the law firm.
D) If the attorney believes it is necessary to prevent a crime or fraud that is likely to result in substantial financial harm.

Answer 57: B
Explanation: Under the Model Rules, an attorney may reveal a client's confidential information without the client's informed consent if the attorney believes it is necessary to defend the attorney against a malpractice claim. Option B reflects the exception to the duty of confidentiality.

Question 58

Attorney Zach is representing a client in a civil lawsuit. During the trial, Zach becomes aware that the opposing counsel is presenting false evidence to the court. What is Zach's ethical duty under the Model Rules of Professional Conduct?

A) Zach must advise the opposing counsel to correct the false evidence.
B) Zach should not take any action, as it is the opposing counsel's responsibility to present evidence.
C) Zach may use the false evidence to his client's advantage.
D) Zach must disclose the false evidence to the court and opposing counsel.

Answer 58: D
Explanation: According to the Model Rules, Attorney Zach's ethical duty is to disclose the false evidence to the court and opposing counsel. Option D reflects the appropriate ethical response.

Question 59
Under the Model Rules of Professional Conduct, what is the attorney's duty when they discover a conflict of interest with a current client?

A) The attorney should take no action and continue representing both clients.
B) The attorney must promptly disclose the conflict to the client and seek the client's informed consent in writing.
C) The attorney is required to withdraw from the representation immediately.
D) The attorney may continue representing both clients as long as they believe it is in the best interests of both parties.

Answer 59: B
Explanation: Under the Model Rules, when an attorney discovers a conflict of interest with a current client, the attorney must promptly disclose the conflict to the client and seek the client's informed consent in writing. Option B reflects the appropriate ethical response.

Question 60
Attorney Xavier is representing a client in a personal injury lawsuit. The client demands that Xavier disclose the client's confidential settlement offer to the opposing party. What should Xavier do under the Model Rules of Professional Conduct?

A) Xavier may disclose the settlement offer as long as the client insists.
B) Xavier should disclose the settlement offer to maintain a transparent process.
C) Xavier is required to advise the client against disclosing the offer and should consider withdrawing from the representation if the client insists.
D) Xavier should disclose the settlement offer to protect the attorney-client privilege.

Answer 60: C
Explanation: According to the Model Rules, Attorney Xavier is required to advise the client against disclosing the settlement offer and should consider withdrawing from the representation if the client insists. This upholds ethical standards and professional integrity.

Question 61

Under the Model Rules of Professional Conduct, what is an attorney's duty when they discover a conflict of interest with a current client?

A) The attorney should take no action and continue representing both clients.
B) The attorney must promptly disclose the conflict to the client and seek the client's informed consent in writing.
C) The attorney is required to withdraw from the representation immediately.
D) The attorney may continue representing both clients as long as they believe it is in the best interests of both parties.

Answer 61: B

Explanation: Under the Model Rules, when an attorney discovers a conflict of interest with a current client, the attorney must promptly disclose the conflict to the client and seek the client's informed consent in writing. Option B reflects the appropriate ethical response.

Question 62

Attorney Yasmine is representing a client in a criminal trial. The client intends to testify falsely in their own defense. What is Yasmine's ethical duty under the Model Rules of Professional Conduct?

A) Yasmine must advise the client to testify truthfully, but if the client insists on testifying falsely, Yasmine may assist in presenting the false testimony.
B) Yasmine should not take any action, as it is the client's decision whether to testify falsely.
C) Yasmine may assist the client in testifying falsely as long as it is relevant to the case.
D) Yasmine must advise the client not to testify falsely and seek permission to withdraw from the representation if necessary.

Answer 62: D

Explanation: According to the Model Rules, Attorney Yasmine's ethical duty is to advise the client not to testify falsely and, if necessary, seek permission to withdraw from the representation. Option D reflects the appropriate ethical response.

Question 63

Under the Model Rules of Professional Conduct, what is an attorney's duty when they discover a conflict of interest with a current client?

A) The attorney should take no action and continue representing both clients.
B) The attorney must promptly disclose the conflict to the client and seek the client's informed consent in writing.
C) The attorney is required to withdraw from the representation immediately.
D) The attorney may continue representing both clients as long as they believe it is in the best interests of both parties.

Answer 63: B

Explanation: Under the Model Rules, when an attorney discovers a conflict of interest with a current client, the attorney must promptly disclose the conflict to the client and seek the client's informed consent in writing. Option B reflects the appropriate ethical response.

Question 64

Attorney Zach is representing a client in a civil lawsuit. During the trial, Zach becomes aware that the opposing counsel is presenting false evidence to the court. What is Zach's ethical duty under the Model Rules of Professional Conduct?

A) Zach must advise the opposing counsel to correct the false evidence.
B) Zach should not take any action, as it is the opposing counsel's responsibility to present evidence.
C) Zach may use the false evidence to his client's advantage.
D) Zach must disclose the false evidence to the court and opposing counsel.

Answer 64: D

Explanation: According to the Model Rules, Attorney Zach's ethical duty is to disclose the false evidence to the court and opposing counsel. Option D reflects the appropriate ethical response.

Question 65

Under the Model Rules of Professional Conduct, what is the attorney's duty when they receive a document that they know was inadvertently sent to them by opposing counsel, and the document contains confidential information of the opposing party?

A) The attorney must return the document without reading it.
B) The attorney may keep the document and use the confidential information if it benefits their client.
C) The attorney must notify opposing counsel and return the document without using or disclosing the confidential information.
D) The attorney should wait for opposing counsel to request the return of the document.

Answer 65: C
Explanation: The attorney's duty, according to the Model Rules, is to promptly notify opposing counsel and return the document without using or disclosing the confidential information. This upholds the duty to protect attorney-client privilege and professional ethics.

Question 66

Attorney William is representing a client in a civil case. During the trial, William becomes aware that the opposing counsel is presenting false evidence to the court. What is William's ethical duty under the Model Rules of Professional Conduct?

A) William must advise the opposing counsel to correct the false evidence.
B) William should not take any action, as it is the opposing counsel's responsibility to present evidence.
C) William may use the false evidence to his client's advantage.
D) William must disclose the false evidence to the court and opposing counsel.

Answer 66: D
Explanation: According to the Model Rules, Attorney William's ethical duty is to disclose the false evidence to the court and opposing counsel. Option D reflects the appropriate ethical response.

Question 67

Under the Model Rules of Professional Conduct, what is the attorney's duty when they receive a document that they know was inadvertently sent to them by opposing counsel, and the document contains confidential information of the opposing party?

A) The attorney must return the document without reading it.
B) The attorney may keep the document and use the confidential information if it benefits their client.
C) The attorney must notify opposing counsel and return the document without using or disclosing the confidential information.
D) The attorney should wait for opposing counsel to request the return of the document.

Answer 67: C

Explanation: The attorney's duty, according to the Model Rules, is to promptly notify opposing counsel and return the document without using or disclosing the confidential information. This upholds the duty to protect attorney-client privilege and professional ethics.

Question 68

Attorney Xavier is representing a client in a personal injury lawsuit. The client demands that Xavier disclose the client's confidential settlement offer to the opposing party. What should Xavier do under the Model Rules of Professional Conduct?

A) Xavier may disclose the settlement offer as long as the client insists.
B) Xavier should disclose the settlement offer to maintain a transparent process.
C) Xavier is required to advise the client against disclosing the offer and should consider withdrawing from the representation if the client insists.
D) Xavier should disclose the settlement offer to protect the attorney-client privilege.

Answer 68: C

Explanation: According to the Model Rules, Attorney Xavier is required to advise the client against disclosing the settlement offer and should consider withdrawing from the representation if the client insists. This upholds ethical standards and professional integrity.

Question 69

Under the Model Rules of Professional Conduct, what is the attorney's duty when they receive a document that they know was inadvertently sent to them by opposing counsel, and the document contains confidential information of the opposing party?

A) The attorney must return the document without reading it.
B) The attorney may keep the document and use the confidential information if it benefits their client.
C) The attorney must notify opposing counsel and return the document without using or disclosing the confidential information.
D) The attorney should wait for opposing counsel to request the return of the document.

Answer 69: C
Explanation: The attorney's duty, according to the Model Rules, is to promptly notify opposing counsel and return the document without using or disclosing the confidential information. This upholds the duty to protect attorney-client privilege and professional ethics.

Question 70

Attorney Sam is representing a client in a criminal case. The client intends to provide false testimony but has not disclosed this to Sam. What is Sam's ethical duty according to the Model Rules of Professional Conduct?

A) Sam should not take any action and proceed with the representation.
B) Sam must advise the client not to provide false testimony if the issue arises during the trial.
C) Sam should immediately withdraw from the representation to avoid potential ethical violations.
D) Sam should assist the client in providing false testimony to secure a favorable outcome.

Answer 70: B
Explanation: According to the Model Rules, Attorney Sam's ethical duty is to advise the client not to provide false testimony if the issue arises during the trial. Option B reflects the appropriate ethical response.

Question 71

Under the Model Rules of Professional Conduct, what is the attorney's duty regarding conflicts of interest involving current clients?

A) The attorney should disclose the conflict to the client and continue representing both clients.
B) The attorney is required to withdraw from the representation of both clients.
C) The attorney may continue representing both clients as long as they are in separate matters.
D) The attorney should seek the informed consent of both clients in writing before proceeding.

Answer 71: B

Explanation: Under the Model Rules, when a conflict of interest arises involving current clients, the attorney is required to withdraw from the representation of both clients. Option B reflects the appropriate ethical response.

Question 72

Attorney Rachel receives a settlement offer from opposing counsel but fails to promptly communicate it to her client. Under the Model Rules of Professional Conduct, what is Rachel's ethical duty?

A) Rachel must immediately withdraw from the representation due to her failure to communicate the offer.
B) Rachel should continue representing her client without disclosing the offer.
C) Rachel must promptly communicate the settlement offer to her client.
D) Rachel may communicate the offer to her client only if it is favorable.

Answer 72: C

Explanation: According to the Model Rules, Attorney Rachel's ethical duty is to promptly communicate the settlement offer to her client. Option C reflects the appropriate ethical response.

Question 73

Under the Model Rules of Professional Conduct, which of the following best describes the duty of an attorney when it comes to the handling of client funds?

A) The attorney may commingle client funds with their personal funds if it is more convenient.
B) The attorney should deposit client funds into a trust account separate from the attorney's personal and business accounts.
C) The attorney is not responsible for keeping records of client funds received.
D) The attorney may use client funds for personal expenses as long as they intend to replenish them later.

Answer 73: B
Explanation: The Model Rules require attorneys to deposit client funds into a trust account separate from the attorney's personal and business accounts to protect client interests. Option B reflects the correct ethical duty.

Question 74

Attorney Victor receives a retainer from a client for legal services to be provided in the future. According to the Model Rules of Professional Conduct, what should Victor do with the retainer?

A) Victor may use the retainer for any personal expenses.
B) Victor should deposit the retainer into a trust account and withdraw it as fees are earned.
C) Victor is not required to keep the retainer in a separate account.
D) Victor may use the retainer for any business expenses related to the law firm.

Answer 74: B
Explanation: Under the Model Rules, Attorney Victor should deposit the retainer into a trust account and withdraw it as fees are earned to protect the client's interests. Option B reflects the appropriate ethical duty.

Question 75

Attorney Emma is representing a client in a criminal case. The client insists on testifying falsely during the trial. What should Emma do under the Model Rules of Professional Conduct?

A) Emma must advise the client to testify truthfully, but if the client insists on testifying falsely, Emma may assist in presenting the false testimony.
B) Emma should not take any action, as it is the client's decision whether to testify falsely.
C) Emma may assist the client in testifying falsely as long as it is relevant to the case.
D) Emma must advise the client not to testify falsely and, if necessary, seek permission to withdraw from the representation.

Answer 75: D
Explanation: According to the Model Rules, Attorney Emma's ethical duty is to advise the client not to testify falsely and, if necessary, seek permission to withdraw from the representation. Option D reflects the appropriate ethical response.

Question 76

Under the Model Rules of Professional Conduct, what is the attorney's duty when they discover a conflict of interest with a current client?

A) The attorney should take no action and continue representing both clients.
B) The attorney must promptly disclose the conflict to the client and seek the client's informed consent in writing.
C) The attorney is required to withdraw from the representation immediately.
D) The attorney may continue representing both clients as long as they believe it is in the best interests of both parties.

Answer 76: B
Explanation: Under the Model Rules, when an attorney discovers a conflict of interest with a current client, the attorney must promptly disclose the conflict to the client and seek the client's informed consent in writing. Option B reflects the appropriate ethical response.

Question 77

Attorney Oliver is representing a client in a personal injury lawsuit. The client insists on disclosing confidential settlement offers to the opposing party without Oliver's consent. What should Oliver do under the Model Rules of Professional Conduct?

A) Oliver should promptly communicate the client's wishes to the opposing party.
B) Oliver must advise the client against disclosing the settlement offers and consider withdrawing from the representation if the client insists.
C) Oliver is required to disclose the settlement offers as per the client's instructions.
D) Oliver may disclose the settlement offers only if they benefit the client's case.

Answer 77: B
Explanation: According to the Model Rules, Attorney Oliver must advise the client against disclosing the settlement offers and consider withdrawing from the representation if the client insists. Option B reflects the appropriate ethical response.

Question 78

Under the Model Rules of Professional Conduct, what is an attorney's duty when they receive a document that they know was inadvertently sent to them by opposing counsel, and the document contains confidential information of the opposing party?

A) The attorney may keep the document and use the confidential information if it benefits their client.
B) The attorney must return the document without reading it.
C) The attorney is required to notify opposing counsel and return the document without using or disclosing the confidential information.
D) The attorney should wait for opposing counsel to request the return of the document.

Answer 78: C
Explanation: The attorney's duty, according to the Model Rules, is to promptly notify opposing counsel and return the document without using or disclosing the confidential information. This upholds the duty to protect attorney-client privilege and professional ethics.

Question 79

Attorney Natalie is representing a client in a criminal trial. The client intends to testify falsely in their own defense. What is Natalie's ethical duty under the Model Rules of Professional Conduct?

A) Natalie must advise the client to testify truthfully, but if the client insists on testifying falsely, Natalie may assist in presenting the false testimony.
B) Natalie should not take any action, as it is the client's decision whether to testify falsely.
C) Natalie may assist the client in testifying falsely as long as it is relevant to the case.
D) Natalie must advise the client not to testify falsely and, if necessary, seek permission to withdraw from the representation.

Answer 79: D
Explanation: According to the Model Rules, Attorney Natalie's ethical duty is to advise the client not to testify falsely and, if necessary, seek permission to withdraw from the representation. Option D reflects the appropriate ethical response.

Question 80

Under the Model Rules of Professional Conduct, what is the attorney's duty regarding conflicts of interest involving current clients?

A) The attorney should disclose the conflict to the client and continue representing both clients.
B) The attorney is required to withdraw from the representation of both clients.
C) The attorney may continue representing both clients as long as they are in separate matters.
D) The attorney should seek the informed consent of both clients in writing before proceeding.

Answer 80: B
Explanation: Under the Model Rules, when a conflict of interest arises involving current clients, the attorney is required to withdraw from the representation of both clients. Option B reflects the appropriate ethical response.

Question 81

Attorney Lisa receives a settlement offer from opposing counsel but fails to promptly communicate it to her client. Under the Model Rules of Professional Conduct, what is Lisa's ethical duty?

A) Lisa must immediately withdraw from the representation due to her failure to communicate the offer.
B) Lisa should continue representing her client without disclosing the offer.
C) Lisa must promptly communicate the settlement offer to her client.
D) Lisa may communicate the offer to her client only if it is favorable.

Answer 81: C
Explanation: According to the Model Rules, Attorney Lisa's ethical duty is to promptly communicate the settlement offer to her client. Option C reflects the appropriate ethical duty.

Question 82

Under the Model Rules of Professional Conduct, which of the following best describes the duty of an attorney when it comes to the handling of client funds?

A) The attorney may commingle client funds with their personal funds if it is more convenient.
B) The attorney should deposit client funds into a trust account separate from the attorney's personal and business accounts.
C) The attorney is not responsible for keeping records of client funds received.
D) The attorney may use client funds for personal expenses as long as they intend to replenish them later.

Answer 82: B
Explanation: The Model Rules require attorneys to deposit client funds into a trust account separate from the attorney's personal and business accounts to protect client interests. Option B reflects the correct ethical duty.

Question 83

Attorney Victor receives a retainer from a client for legal services to be provided in the future. According to the Model Rules of Professional Conduct, what should Victor do with the retainer?

A) Victor may use the retainer for any personal expenses.
B) Victor should deposit the retainer into a trust account and withdraw it as fees are earned.
C) Victor is not required to keep the retainer in a separate account.
D) Victor may use the retainer for any business expenses related to the law firm.

Answer 83: B

Explanation: Under the Model Rules, Attorney Victor should deposit the retainer into a trust account and withdraw it as fees are earned to protect the client's interests. Option B reflects the appropriate ethical duty.

Question 84

Attorney Emma is representing a client in a criminal case. The client insists on testifying falsely during the trial. What should Emma do under the Model Rules of Professional Conduct?

A) Emma must advise the client to testify truthfully, but if the client insists on testifying falsely, Emma may assist in presenting the false testimony.
B) Emma should not take any action, as it is the client's decision whether to testify falsely.
C) Emma may assist the client in testifying falsely as long as it is relevant to the case.
D) Emma must advise the client not to testify falsely and, if necessary, seek permission to withdraw from the representation.

Answer 84: D

Explanation: According to the Model Rules, Attorney Emma's ethical duty is to advise the client not to testify falsely and, if necessary, seek permission to withdraw from the representation. Option D reflects the appropriate ethical response.

Question 85

Under the Model Rules of Professional Conduct, what is the attorney's duty regarding conflicts of interest involving current clients?

A) The attorney should disclose the conflict to the client and continue representing both clients.
B) The attorney is required to withdraw from the representation of both clients.
C) The attorney may continue representing both clients as long as they are in separate matters.
D) The attorney should seek the informed consent of both clients in writing before proceeding.

Answer 85: B

Explanation: Under the Model Rules, when a conflict of interest arises involving current clients, the attorney is required to withdraw from the representation of both clients. Option B reflects the appropriate ethical response.

Question 86

Attorney Rachel receives a settlement offer from opposing counsel but fails to promptly communicate it to her client. Under the Model Rules of Professional Conduct, what is Rachel's ethical duty?

A) Rachel must immediately withdraw from the representation due to her failure to communicate the offer.
B) Rachel should continue representing her client without disclosing the offer.
C) Rachel must promptly communicate the settlement offer to her client.
D) Rachel may communicate the offer to her client only if it is favorable.

Answer 86: C

Explanation: According to the Model Rules, Attorney Rachel's ethical duty is to promptly communicate the settlement offer to her client. Option C reflects the appropriate ethical duty.

Question 87

Under the Model Rules of Professional Conduct, which of the following best describes the duty of an attorney when it comes to the handling of client funds?

A) The attorney may commingle client funds with their personal funds if it is more convenient.
B) The attorney should deposit client funds into a trust account separate from the attorney's personal and business accounts.
C) The attorney is not responsible for keeping records of client funds received.
D) The attorney may use client funds for personal expenses as long as they intend to replenish them later.

Answer 87: B

Explanation: The Model Rules require attorneys to deposit client funds into a trust account separate from the attorney's personal and business accounts to protect client interests. Option B reflects the correct ethical duty.

Question 88

Attorney Victor receives a retainer from a client for legal services to be provided in the future. According to the Model Rules of Professional Conduct, what should Victor do with the retainer?

A) Victor may use the retainer for any personal expenses.
B) Victor should deposit the retainer into a trust account and withdraw it as fees are earned.
C) Victor is not required to keep the retainer in a separate account.
D) Victor may use the retainer for any business expenses related to the law firm.

Answer 88: B

Explanation: Under the Model Rules, Attorney Victor should deposit the retainer into a trust account and withdraw it as fees are earned to protect the client's interests. Option B reflects the appropriate ethical duty.

Question 89

Attorney Emma is representing a client in a criminal case. The client insists on testifying falsely during the trial. What should Emma do under the Model Rules of Professional Conduct?

A) Emma must advise the client to testify truthfully, but if the client insists on testifying falsely, Emma may assist in presenting the false testimony.
B) Emma should not take any action, as it is the client's decision whether to testify falsely.
C) Emma may assist the client in testifying falsely as long as it is relevant to the case.
D) Emma must advise the client not to testify falsely and, if necessary, seek permission to withdraw from the representation.

Answer 89: D
Explanation: According to the Model Rules, Attorney Emma's ethical duty is to advise the client not to testify falsely and, if necessary, seek permission to withdraw from the representation. Option D reflects the appropriate ethical response.

Question 90

Under the Model Rules of Professional Conduct, what is the attorney's duty regarding conflicts of interest involving current clients?

A) The attorney should disclose the conflict to the client and continue representing both clients.
B) The attorney is required to withdraw from the representation of both clients.
C) The attorney may continue representing both clients as long as they are in separate matters.
D) The attorney should seek the informed consent of both clients in writing before proceeding.

Answer 90: B
Explanation: Under the Model Rules, when a conflict of interest arises involving current clients, the attorney is required to withdraw from the representation of both clients. Option B reflects the appropriate ethical response.

Question 91

Attorney Lisa receives a settlement offer from opposing counsel but fails to promptly communicate it to her client. Under the Model Rules of Professional Conduct, what is Lisa's ethical duty?

A) Lisa must immediately withdraw from the representation due to her failure to communicate the offer.
B) Lisa should continue representing her client without disclosing the offer.
C) Lisa must promptly communicate the settlement offer to her client.
D) Lisa may communicate the offer to her client only if it is favorable.

Answer 91: C

Explanation: According to the Model Rules, Attorney Lisa's ethical duty is to promptly communicate the settlement offer to her client. Option C reflects the appropriate ethical duty.

Question 92

Under the Model Rules of Professional Conduct, which of the following best describes the duty of an attorney when it comes to the handling of client funds?

A) The attorney may commingle client funds with their personal funds if it is more convenient.
B) The attorney should deposit client funds into a trust account separate from the attorney's personal and business accounts.
C) The attorney is not responsible for keeping records of client funds received.
D) The attorney may use client funds for personal expenses as long as they intend to replenish them later.

Answer 92: B

Explanation: The Model Rules require attorneys to deposit client funds into a trust account separate from the attorney's personal and business accounts to protect client interests. Option B reflects the correct ethical duty.

Question 93

Attorney Victor receives a retainer from a client for legal services to be provided in the future. According to the Model Rules of Professional Conduct, what should Victor do with the retainer?

A) Victor may use the retainer for any personal expenses.
B) Victor should deposit the retainer into a trust account and withdraw it as fees are earned.
C) Victor is not required to keep the retainer in a separate account.
D) Victor may use the retainer for any business expenses related to the law firm.

Answer 93: B
Explanation: Under the Model Rules, Attorney Victor should deposit the retainer into a trust account and withdraw it as fees are earned to protect the client's interests. Option B reflects the appropriate ethical duty.

Question 94

Attorney Emma is representing a client in a criminal case. The client insists on testifying falsely during the trial. What should Emma do under the Model Rules of Professional Conduct?

A) Emma must advise the client to testify truthfully, but if the client insists on testifying falsely, Emma may assist in presenting the false testimony.
B) Emma should not take any action, as it is the client's decision whether to testify falsely.
C) Emma may assist the client in testifying falsely as long as it is relevant to the case.
D) Emma must advise the client not to testify falsely and, if necessary, seek permission to withdraw from the representation.

Answer 94: D
Explanation: According to the Model Rules, Attorney Emma's ethical duty is to advise the client not to testify falsely and, if necessary, seek permission to withdraw from the representation. Option D reflects the appropriate ethical response.

Question 95

Under the Model Rules of Professional Conduct, what is the attorney's duty regarding conflicts of interest involving current clients?

A) The attorney should disclose the conflict to the client and continue representing both clients.
B) The attorney is required to withdraw from the representation of both clients.
C) The attorney may continue representing both clients as long as they are in separate matters.
D) The attorney should seek the informed consent of both clients in writing before proceeding.

Answer 95: B

Explanation: Under the Model Rules, when a conflict of interest arises involving current clients, the attorney is required to withdraw from the representation of both clients. Option B reflects the appropriate ethical response.

Question 96

Attorney Rachel receives a settlement offer from opposing counsel but fails to promptly communicate it to her client. Under the Model Rules of Professional Conduct, what is Rachel's ethical duty?

A) Rachel must immediately withdraw from the representation due to her failure to communicate the offer.
B) Rachel should continue representing her client without disclosing the offer.
C) Rachel must promptly communicate the settlement offer to her client.
D) Rachel may communicate the offer to her client only if it is favorable.

Answer 96: C

Explanation: According to the Model Rules, Attorney Rachel's ethical duty is to promptly communicate the settlement offer to her client. Option C reflects the appropriate ethical duty.

Question 97
Under the Model Rules of Professional Conduct, which of the following best describes the duty of an attorney when it comes to the handling of client funds?

A) The attorney may commingle client funds with their personal funds if it is more convenient.
B) The attorney should deposit client funds into a trust account separate from the attorney's personal and business accounts.
C) The attorney is not responsible for keeping records of client funds received.
D) The attorney may use client funds for personal expenses as long as they intend to replenish them later.

Answer 97: B
Explanation: The Model Rules require attorneys to deposit client funds into a trust account separate from the attorney's personal and business accounts to protect client interests. Option B reflects the correct ethical duty.

Question 98
Attorney Victor receives a retainer from a client for legal services to be provided in the future. According to the Model Rules of Professional Conduct, what should Victor do with the retainer?

A) Victor may use the retainer for any personal expenses.
B) Victor should deposit the retainer into a trust account and withdraw it as fees are earned.
C) Victor is not required to keep the retainer in a separate account.
D) Victor may use the retainer for any business expenses related to the law firm.

Answer 98: B
Explanation: Under the Model Rules, Attorney Victor should deposit the retainer into a trust account and withdraw it as fees are earned to protect the client's interests. Option B reflects the appropriate ethical duty.

Question 99

Attorney Emma is representing a client in a criminal case. The client insists on testifying falsely during the trial. What should Emma do under the Model Rules of Professional Conduct?

A) Emma must advise the client to testify truthfully, but if the client insists on testifying falsely, Emma may assist in presenting the false testimony.
B) Emma should not take any action, as it is the client's decision whether to testify falsely.
C) Emma may assist the client in testifying falsely as long as it is relevant to the case.
D) Emma must advise the client not to testify falsely and, if necessary, seek permission to withdraw from the representation.

Answer 99: D
Explanation: According to the Model Rules, Attorney Emma's ethical duty is to advise the client not to testify falsely and, if necessary, seek permission to withdraw from the representation. Option D reflects the appropriate ethical response.

Question 100

Under the Model Rules of Professional Conduct, what is the attorney's duty regarding conflicts of interest involving current clients?

A) The attorney should disclose the conflict to the client and continue representing both clients.
B) The attorney is required to withdraw from the representation of both clients.
C) The attorney may continue representing both clients as long as they are in separate matters.
D) The attorney should seek the informed consent of both clients in writing before proceeding.

Answer 100: B
Explanation: Under the Model Rules, when a conflict of interest arises involving current clients, the attorney is required to withdraw from the representation of both clients. Option B reflects the appropriate ethical response.

Question 101

Under the Model Rules of Professional Conduct, what is the attorney's duty regarding conflicts of interest involving current clients?

A) The attorney should disclose the conflict to the client and continue representing both clients.
B) The attorney is required to withdraw from the representation of both clients.
C) The attorney may continue representing both clients as long as they are in separate matters.
D) The attorney should seek the informed consent of both clients in writing before proceeding.

Answer 101: B
Explanation: Under the Model Rules, when a conflict of interest arises involving current clients, the attorney is required to withdraw from the representation of both clients. Option B reflects the appropriate ethical response.

Question 102

Attorney Lisa receives a settlement offer from opposing counsel but fails to promptly communicate it to her client. Under the Model Rules of Professional Conduct, what is Lisa's ethical duty?

A) Lisa must immediately withdraw from the representation due to her failure to communicate the offer.
B) Lisa should continue representing her client without disclosing the offer.
C) Lisa must promptly communicate the settlement offer to her client.
D) Lisa may communicate the offer to her client only if it is favorable.

Answer 102: C
Explanation: According to the Model Rules, Attorney Lisa's ethical duty is to promptly communicate the settlement offer to her client. Option C reflects the appropriate ethical duty.

Question 103

Under the Model Rules of Professional Conduct, which of the following best describes the duty of an attorney when it comes to the handling of client funds?

A) The attorney may commingle client funds with their personal funds if it is more convenient.
B) The attorney should deposit client funds into a trust account separate from the attorney's personal and business accounts.
C) The attorney is not responsible for keeping records of client funds received.
D) The attorney may use client funds for personal expenses as long as they intend to replenish them later.

Answer 103: B

Explanation: The Model Rules require attorneys to deposit client funds into a trust account separate from the attorney's personal and business accounts to protect client interests. Option B reflects the correct ethical duty.

Question 104

Attorney Victor receives a retainer from a client for legal services to be provided in the future. According to the Model Rules of Professional Conduct, what should Victor do with the retainer?

A) Victor may use the retainer for any personal expenses.
B) Victor should deposit the retainer into a trust account and withdraw it as fees are earned.
C) Victor is not required to keep the retainer in a separate account.
D) Victor may use the retainer for any business expenses related to the law firm.

Answer 104: B

Explanation: Under the Model Rules, Attorney Victor should deposit the retainer into a trust account and withdraw it as fees are earned to protect the client's interests. Option B reflects the appropriate ethical duty.

Question 105

Attorney Emma is representing a client in a criminal case. The client insists on testifying falsely during the trial. What should Emma do under the Model Rules of Professional Conduct?

A) Emma must advise the client to testify truthfully, but if the client insists on testifying falsely, Emma may assist in presenting the false testimony.
B) Emma should not take any action, as it is the client's decision whether to testify falsely.
C) Emma may assist the client in testifying falsely as long as it is relevant to the case.
D) Emma must advise the client not to testify falsely and, if necessary, seek permission to withdraw from the representation.

Answer 105: D
Explanation: According to the Model Rules, Attorney Emma's ethical duty is to advise the client not to testify falsely and, if necessary, seek permission to withdraw from the representation. Option D reflects the appropriate ethical response.

Question 106

Under the Model Rules of Professional Conduct, what is the attorney's duty regarding conflicts of interest involving current clients?

A) The attorney should disclose the conflict to the client and continue representing both clients.
B) The attorney is required to withdraw from the representation of both clients.
C) The attorney may continue representing both clients as long as they are in separate matters.
D) The attorney should seek the informed consent of both clients in writing before proceeding.

Answer 106: B
Explanation: Under the Model Rules, when a conflict of interest arises involving current clients, the attorney is required to withdraw from the representation of both clients. Option B reflects the appropriate ethical response.

Question 107

Attorney Rachel receives a settlement offer from opposing counsel but fails to promptly communicate it to her client. Under the Model Rules of Professional Conduct, what is Rachel's ethical duty?

A) Rachel must immediately withdraw from the representation due to her failure to communicate the offer.
B) Rachel should continue representing her client without disclosing the offer.
C) Rachel must promptly communicate the settlement offer to her client.
D) Rachel may communicate the offer to her client only if it is favorable.

Answer 107: C
Explanation: According to the Model Rules, Attorney Rachel's ethical duty is to promptly communicate the settlement offer to her client. Option C reflects the appropriate ethical duty.

Question 108

Under the Model Rules of Professional Conduct, which of the following best describes the duty of an attorney when it comes to the handling of client funds?

A) The attorney may commingle client funds with their personal funds if it is more convenient.
B) The attorney should deposit client funds into a trust account separate from the attorney's personal and business accounts.
C) The attorney is not responsible for keeping records of client funds received.
D) The attorney may use client funds for personal expenses as long as they intend to replenish them later.

Answer 108: B
Explanation: The Model Rules require attorneys to deposit client funds into a trust account separate from the attorney's personal and business accounts to protect client interests. Option B reflects the correct ethical duty.

Question 109
Attorney Victor receives a retainer from a client for legal services to be provided in the future. According to the Model Rules of Professional Conduct, what should Victor do with the retainer?

A) Victor may use the retainer for any personal expenses.
B) Victor should deposit the retainer into a trust account and withdraw it as fees are earned.
C) Victor is not required to keep the retainer in a separate account.
D) Victor may use the retainer for any business expenses related to the law firm.

Answer 109: B
Explanation: Under the Model Rules, Attorney Victor should deposit the retainer into a trust account and withdraw it as fees are earned to protect the client's interests. Option B reflects the appropriate ethical duty.

Question 110
Attorney Emma is representing a client in a criminal case. The client insists on testifying falsely during the trial. What should Emma do under the Model Rules of Professional Conduct?

A) Emma must advise the client to testify truthfully, but if the client insists on testifying falsely, Emma may assist in presenting the false testimony.
B) Emma should not take any action, as it is the client's decision whether to testify falsely.
C) Emma may assist the client in testifying falsely as long as it is relevant to the case.
D) Emma must advise the client not to testify falsely and, if necessary, seek permission to withdraw from the representation.

Answer 110: D
Explanation: According to the Model Rules, Attorney Emma's ethical duty is to advise the client not to testify falsely and, if necessary, seek permission to withdraw from the representation. Option D reflects the appropriate ethical response.

Question 111

Under the Model Rules of Professional Conduct, what is the attorney's duty regarding conflicts of interest involving current clients?

A) The attorney should disclose the conflict to the client and continue representing both clients.
B) The attorney is required to withdraw from the representation of both clients.
C) The attorney may continue representing both clients as long as they are in separate matters.
D) The attorney should seek the informed consent of both clients in writing before proceeding.

Answer 111: B
Explanation: Under the Model Rules, when a conflict of interest arises involving current clients, the attorney is required to withdraw from the representation of both clients. Option B reflects the appropriate ethical response.

Question 112

Attorney Lisa receives a settlement offer from opposing counsel but fails to promptly communicate it to her client. Under the Model Rules of Professional Conduct, what is Lisa's ethical duty?

A) Lisa must immediately withdraw from the representation due to her failure to communicate the offer.
B) Lisa should continue representing her client without disclosing the offer.
C) Lisa must promptly communicate the settlement offer to her client.
D) Lisa may communicate the offer to her client only if it is favorable.

Answer 112: C
Explanation: According to the Model Rules, Attorney Lisa's ethical duty is to promptly communicate the settlement offer to her client. Option C reflects the appropriate ethical duty.

Question 113

Under the Model Rules of Professional Conduct, which of the following best describes the duty of an attorney when it comes to the handling of client funds?

A) The attorney may commingle client funds with their personal funds if it is more convenient.
B) The attorney should deposit client funds into a trust account separate from the attorney's personal and business accounts.
C) The attorney is not responsible for keeping records of client funds received.
D) The attorney may use client funds for personal expenses as long as they intend to replenish them later.

Answer 113: B
Explanation: The Model Rules require attorneys to deposit client funds into a trust account separate from the attorney's personal and business accounts to protect client interests. Option B reflects the correct ethical duty.

Question 114

Attorney Victor receives a retainer from a client for legal services to be provided in the future. According to the Model Rules of Professional Conduct, what should Victor do with the retainer?

A) Victor may use the retainer for any personal expenses.
B) Victor should deposit the retainer into a trust account and withdraw it as fees are earned.
C) Victor is not required to keep the retainer in a separate account.
D) Victor may use the retainer for any business expenses related to the law firm.

Answer 114: B
Explanation: Under the Model Rules, Attorney Victor should deposit the retainer into a trust account and withdraw it as fees are earned to protect the client's interests. Option B reflects the appropriate ethical duty.

Question 115

Attorney Emma is representing a client in a criminal case. The client insists on testifying falsely during the trial. What should Emma do under the Model Rules of Professional Conduct?

A) Emma must advise the client to testify truthfully, but if the client insists on testifying falsely, Emma may assist in presenting the false testimony.
B) Emma should not take any action, as it is the client's decision whether to testify falsely.
C) Emma may assist the client in testifying falsely as long as it is relevant to the case.
D) Emma must advise the client not to testify falsely and, if necessary, seek permission to withdraw from the representation.

Answer 115: D
Explanation: According to the Model Rules, Attorney Emma's ethical duty is to advise the client not to testify falsely and, if necessary, seek permission to withdraw from the representation. Option D reflects the appropriate ethical response.

Question 116

Under the Model Rules of Professional Conduct, what is the attorney's duty regarding conflicts of interest involving current clients?

A) The attorney should disclose the conflict to the client and continue representing both clients.
B) The attorney is required to withdraw from the representation of both clients.
C) The attorney may continue representing both clients as long as they are in separate matters.
D) The attorney should seek the informed consent of both clients in writing before proceeding.

Answer 116: B
Explanation: Under the Model Rules, when a conflict of interest arises involving current clients, the attorney is required to withdraw from the representation of both clients. Option B reflects the appropriate ethical response.

Question 117
Attorney Rachel receives a settlement offer from opposing counsel but fails to promptly communicate it to her client. Under the Model Rules of Professional Conduct, what is Rachel's ethical duty?

A) Rachel must immediately withdraw from the representation due to her failure to communicate the offer.
B) Rachel should continue representing her client without disclosing the offer.
C) Rachel must promptly communicate the settlement offer to her client.
D) Rachel may communicate the offer to her client only if it is favorable.

Answer 117: C
Explanation: According to the Model Rules, Attorney Rachel's ethical duty is to promptly communicate the settlement offer to her client. Option C reflects the appropriate ethical duty.

Question 118
Under the Model Rules of Professional Conduct, which of the following best describes the duty of an attorney when it comes to the handling of client funds?

A) The attorney may commingle client funds with their personal funds if it is more convenient.
B) The attorney should deposit client funds into a trust account separate from the attorney's personal and business accounts.
C) The attorney is not responsible for keeping records of client funds received.
D) The attorney may use client funds for personal expenses as long as they intend to replenish them later.

Answer 118: B
Explanation: The Model Rules require attorneys to deposit client funds into a trust account separate from the attorney's personal and business accounts to protect client interests. Option B reflects the correct ethical duty.

Question 119
Attorney Victor receives a retainer from a client for legal services to be provided in the future. According to the Model Rules of Professional Conduct, what should Victor do with the retainer?

A) Victor may use the retainer for any personal expenses.

B) Victor should deposit the retainer into a trust account and withdraw it as fees are earned.
C) Victor is not required to keep the retainer in a separate account.
D) Victor may use the retainer for any business expenses related to the law firm.

Answer 119: B
Explanation: Under the Model Rules, Attorney Victor should deposit the retainer into a trust account and withdraw it as fees are earned to protect the client's interests. Option B reflects the appropriate ethical duty.

Question 120
Attorney Emma is representing a client in a criminal case. The client insists on testifying falsely during the trial. What should Emma do under the Model Rules of Professional Conduct?

A) Emma must advise the client to testify truthfully, but if the client insists on testifying falsely, Emma may assist in presenting the false testimony.
B) Emma should not take any action, as it is the client's decision whether to testify falsely.
C) Emma may assist the client in testifying falsely as long as it is relevant to the case.
D) Emma must advise the client not to testify falsely and, if necessary, seek permission to withdraw from the representation.

Answer 120: D
Explanation: According to the Model Rules, Attorney Emma's ethical duty is to advise the client not to testify falsely and, if necessary, seek permission to withdraw from the representation. Option D reflects the appropriate ethical response.

Question 121
Under the Model Rules of Professional Conduct, what is the attorney's duty regarding conflicts of interest involving current clients?

A) The attorney should disclose the conflict to the client and continue representing both clients.
B) The attorney is required to withdraw from the representation of both clients.
C) The attorney may continue representing both clients as long as they are in separate matters.

D) The attorney should seek the informed consent of both clients in writing before proceeding.

Answer 121: B
Explanation: Under the Model Rules, when a conflict of interest arises involving current clients, the attorney is required to withdraw from the representation of both clients. Option B reflects the appropriate ethical response.

Question 122
Attorney Lisa receives a settlement offer from opposing counsel but fails to promptly communicate it to her client. Under the Model Rules of Professional Conduct, what is Lisa's ethical duty?

A) Lisa must immediately withdraw from the representation due to her failure to communicate the offer.
B) Lisa should continue representing her client without disclosing the offer.
C) Lisa must promptly communicate the settlement offer to her client.
D) Lisa may communicate the offer to her client only if it is favorable.

Answer 122: C
Explanation: According to the Model Rules, Attorney Lisa's ethical duty is to promptly communicate the settlement offer to her client. Option C reflects the appropriate ethical duty.

Question 123
Under the Model Rules of Professional Conduct, which of the following best describes the duty of an attorney when it comes to the handling of client funds?

A) The attorney may commingle client funds with their personal funds if it is more convenient.
B) The attorney should deposit client funds into a trust account separate from the attorney's personal and business accounts.
C) The attorney is not responsible for keeping records of client funds received.
D) The attorney may use client funds for personal expenses as long as they intend to replenish them later.

Answer 123: B

Explanation: The Model Rules require attorneys to deposit client funds into a trust account separate from the attorney's personal and business accounts to protect client interests. Option B reflects the correct ethical duty.

Question 124

Attorney Victor receives a retainer from a client for legal services to be provided in the future. According to the Model Rules of Professional Conduct, what should Victor do with the retainer?

A) Victor may use the retainer for any personal expenses.
B) Victor should deposit the retainer into a trust account and withdraw it as fees are earned.
C) Victor is not required to keep the retainer in a separate account.
D) Victor may use the retainer for any business expenses related to the law firm.

Answer 124: B
Explanation: Under the Model Rules, Attorney Victor should deposit the retainer into a trust account and withdraw it as fees are earned to protect the client's interests. Option B reflects the appropriate ethical duty.

Question 125

Attorney Emma is representing a client in a criminal case. The client insists on testifying falsely during the trial. What should Emma do under the Model Rules of Professional Conduct?

A) Emma must advise the client to testify truthfully, but if the client insists on testifying falsely, Emma may assist in presenting the false testimony.
B) Emma should not take any action, as it is the client's decision whether to testify falsely.
C) Emma may assist the client in testifying falsely as long as it is relevant to the case.
D) Emma must advise the client not to testify falsely and, if necessary, seek permission to withdraw from the representation.

Answer 125: D
Explanation: According to the Model Rules, Attorney Emma's ethical duty is to advise the client not to testify falsely and, if necessary, seek permission to withdraw from the representation. Option D reflects the appropriate ethical response.

Question 126
Under the Model Rules of Professional Conduct, what is the attorney's duty regarding conflicts of interest involving current clients?

A) The attorney should disclose the conflict to the client and continue representing both clients.
B) The attorney is required to withdraw from the representation of both clients.
C) The attorney may continue representing both clients as long as they are in separate matters.
D) The attorney should seek the informed consent of both clients in writing before proceeding.

Answer 126: B
Explanation: Under the Model Rules, when a conflict of interest arises involving current clients, the attorney is required to withdraw from the representation of both clients. Option B reflects the appropriate ethical response.

Question 127
Attorney Rachel receives a settlement offer from opposing counsel but fails to promptly communicate it to her client. Under the Model Rules of Professional Conduct, what is Rachel's ethical duty?

A) Rachel must immediately withdraw from the representation due to her failure to communicate the offer.
B) Rachel should continue representing her client without disclosing the offer.
C) Rachel must promptly communicate the settlement offer to her client.
D) Rachel may communicate the offer to her client only if it is favorable.

Answer 127: C
Explanation: According to the Model Rules, Attorney Rachel's ethical duty is to promptly communicate the settlement offer to her client. Option C reflects the appropriate ethical duty.

Question 128

Under the Model Rules of Professional Conduct, which of the following best describes the duty of an attorney when it comes to the handling of client funds?

A) The attorney may commingle client funds with their personal funds if it is more convenient.
B) The attorney should deposit client funds into a trust account separate from the attorney's personal and business accounts.
C) The attorney is not responsible for keeping records of client funds received.
D) The attorney may use client funds for personal expenses as long as they intend to replenish them later.

Answer 128: B

Explanation: The Model Rules require attorneys to deposit client funds into a trust account separate from the attorney's personal and business accounts to protect client interests. Option B reflects the correct ethical duty.

Question 129

Attorney Victor receives a retainer from a client for legal services to be provided in the future. According to the Model Rules of Professional Conduct, what should Victor do with the retainer?

A) Victor may use the retainer for any personal expenses.
B) Victor should deposit the retainer into a trust account and withdraw it as fees are earned.
C) Victor is not required to keep the retainer in a separate account.
D) Victor may use the retainer for any business expenses related to the law firm.

Answer 129: B

Explanation: Under the Model Rules, Attorney Victor should deposit the retainer into a trust account and withdraw it as fees are earned to protect the client's interests. Option B reflects the appropriate ethical duty.

Question 130

Attorney Emma is representing a client in a criminal case. The client insists on testifying falsely during the trial. What should Emma do under the Model Rules of Professional Conduct?

A) Emma must advise the client to testify truthfully, but if the client insists on testifying falsely, Emma may assist in presenting the false testimony.
B) Emma should not take any action, as it is the client's decision whether to testify falsely.
C) Emma may assist the client in testifying falsely as long as it is relevant to the case.
D) Emma must advise the client not to testify falsely and, if necessary, seek permission to withdraw from the representation.

Answer 130: D
Explanation: According to the Model Rules, Attorney Emma's ethical duty is to advise the client not to testify falsely and, if necessary, seek permission to withdraw from the representation. Option D reflects the appropriate ethical response.

Question 131

Under the Model Rules of Professional Conduct, what is the attorney's duty regarding conflicts of interest involving current clients?

A) The attorney should disclose the conflict to the client and continue representing both clients.
B) The attorney is required to withdraw from the representation of both clients.
C) The attorney may continue representing both clients as long as they are in separate matters.
D) The attorney should seek the informed consent of both clients in writing before proceeding.

Answer 131: B
Explanation: Under the Model Rules, when a conflict of interest arises involving current clients, the attorney is required to withdraw from the representation of both clients. Option B reflects the appropriate ethical response.

Question 132

Attorney Lisa receives a settlement offer from opposing counsel but fails to promptly communicate it to her client. Under the Model Rules of Professional Conduct, what is Lisa's ethical duty?

A) Lisa must immediately withdraw from the representation due to her failure to communicate the offer.
B) Lisa should continue representing her client without disclosing the offer.
C) Lisa must promptly communicate the settlement offer to her client.
D) Lisa may communicate the offer to her client only if it is favorable.

Answer 132: C
Explanation: According to the Model Rules, Attorney Lisa's ethical duty is to promptly communicate the settlement offer to her client. Option C reflects the appropriate ethical duty.

Question 133

Under the Model Rules of Professional Conduct, which of the following best describes the duty of an attorney when it comes to the handling of client funds?

A) The attorney may commingle client funds with their personal funds if it is more convenient.
B) The attorney should deposit client funds into a trust account separate from the attorney's personal and business accounts.
C) The attorney is not responsible for keeping records of client funds received.
D) The attorney may use client funds for personal expenses as long as they intend to replenish them later.

Answer 133: B
Explanation: The Model Rules require attorneys to deposit client funds into a trust account separate from the attorney's personal and business accounts to protect client interests. Option B reflects the correct ethical duty.

Question 134

Attorney Victor receives a retainer from a client for legal services to be provided in the future. According to the Model Rules of Professional Conduct, what should Victor do with the retainer?

A) Victor may use the retainer for any personal expenses.
B) Victor should deposit the retainer into a trust account and withdraw it as fees are earned.
C) Victor is not required to keep the retainer in a separate account.
D) Victor may use the retainer for any business expenses related to the law firm.

Answer 134: B
Explanation: Under the Model Rules, Attorney Victor should deposit the retainer into a trust account and withdraw it as fees are earned to protect the client's interests. Option B reflects the appropriate ethical duty.

Question 135

Attorney Emma is representing a client in a criminal case. The client insists on testifying falsely during the trial. What should Emma do under the Model Rules of Professional Conduct?

A) Emma must advise the client to testify truthfully, but if the client insists on testifying falsely, Emma may assist in presenting the false testimony.
B) Emma should not take any action, as it is the client's decision whether to testify falsely.
C) Emma may assist the client in testifying falsely as long as it is relevant to the case.
D) Emma must advise the client not to testify falsely and, if necessary, seek permission to withdraw from the representation.

Answer 135: D
Explanation: According to the Model Rules, Attorney Emma's ethical duty is to advise the client not to testify falsely and, if necessary, seek permission to withdraw from the representation. Option D reflects the appropriate ethical response.

Question 136

Under the Model Rules of Professional Conduct, what is the attorney's duty regarding conflicts of interest involving current clients?

A) The attorney should disclose the conflict to the client and continue representing both clients.
B) The attorney is required to withdraw from the representation of both clients.
C) The attorney may continue representing both clients as long as they are in separate matters.
D) The attorney should seek the informed consent of both clients in writing before proceeding.

Answer 136: B

Explanation: Under the Model Rules, when a conflict of interest arises involving current clients, the attorney is required to withdraw from the representation of both clients. Option B reflects the appropriate ethical response.

Question 137

Attorney Rachel receives a settlement offer from opposing counsel but fails to promptly communicate it to her client. Under the Model Rules of Professional Conduct, what is Rachel's ethical duty?

A) Rachel must immediately withdraw from the representation due to her failure to communicate the offer.
B) Rachel should continue representing her client without disclosing the offer.
C) Rachel must promptly communicate the settlement offer to her client.
D) Rachel may communicate the offer to her client only if it is favorable.

Answer 137: C

Explanation: According to the Model Rules, Attorney Rachel's ethical duty is to promptly communicate the settlement offer to her client. Option C reflects the appropriate ethical duty.

Question 138
Under the Model Rules of Professional Conduct, which of the following best describes the duty of an attorney when it comes to the handling of client funds?

A) The attorney may commingle client funds with their personal funds if it is more convenient.
B) The attorney should deposit client funds into a trust account separate from the attorney's personal and business accounts.
C) The attorney is not responsible for keeping records of client funds received.
D) The attorney may use client funds for personal expenses as long as they intend to replenish them later.

Answer 138: B
Explanation: The Model Rules require attorneys to deposit client funds into a trust account separate from the attorney's personal and business accounts to protect client interests. Option B reflects the correct ethical duty.

Question 139
Attorney Victor receives a retainer from a client for legal services to be provided in the future. According to the Model Rules of Professional Conduct, what should Victor do with the retainer?

A) Victor may use the retainer for any personal expenses.
B) Victor should deposit the retainer into a trust account and withdraw it as fees are earned.
C) Victor is not required to keep the retainer in a separate account.
D) Victor may use the retainer for any business expenses related to the law firm.

Answer 139: B
Explanation: Under the Model Rules, Attorney Victor should deposit the retainer into a trust account and withdraw it as fees are earned to protect the client's interests. Option B reflects the appropriate ethical duty.

Question 140

Attorney Emma is representing a client in a criminal case. The client insists on testifying falsely during the trial. What should Emma do under the Model Rules of Professional Conduct?

A) Emma must advise the client to testify truthfully, but if the client insists on testifying falsely, Emma may assist in presenting the false testimony.
B) Emma should not take any action, as it is the client's decision whether to testify falsely.
C) Emma may assist the client in testifying falsely as long as it is relevant to the case.
D) Emma must advise the client not to testify falsely and, if necessary, seek permission to withdraw from the representation.

Answer 140: D
Explanation: According to the Model Rules, Attorney Emma's ethical duty is to advise the client not to testify falsely and, if necessary, seek permission to withdraw from the representation. Option D reflects the appropriate ethical response.

Question 141

Under the Model Rules of Professional Conduct, what is the attorney's duty regarding conflicts of interest involving current clients?

A) The attorney should disclose the conflict to the client and continue representing both clients.
B) The attorney is required to withdraw from the representation of both clients.
C) The attorney may continue representing both clients as long as they are in separate matters.
D) The attorney should seek the informed consent of both clients in writing before proceeding.

Answer 141: B
Explanation: Under the Model Rules, when a conflict of interest arises involving current clients, the attorney is required to withdraw from the representation of both clients. Option B reflects the appropriate ethical response.

Question 142

Attorney Lisa receives a settlement offer from opposing counsel but fails to promptly communicate it to her client. Under the Model Rules of Professional Conduct, what is Lisa's ethical duty?

A) Lisa must immediately withdraw from the representation due to her failure to communicate the offer.
B) Lisa should continue representing her client without disclosing the offer.
C) Lisa must promptly communicate the settlement offer to her client.
D) Lisa may communicate the offer to her client only if it is favorable.

Answer 142: C
Explanation: According to the Model Rules, Attorney Lisa's ethical duty is to promptly communicate the settlement offer to her client. Option C reflects the appropriate ethical duty.

Question 143

Under the Model Rules of Professional Conduct, which of the following best describes the duty of an attorney when it comes to the handling of client funds?

A) The attorney may commingle client funds with their personal funds if it is more convenient.
B) The attorney should deposit client funds into a trust account separate from the attorney's personal and business accounts.
C) The attorney is not responsible for keeping records of client funds received.
D) The attorney may use client funds for personal expenses as long as they intend to replenish them later.

Answer 143: B
Explanation: The Model Rules require attorneys to deposit client funds into a trust account separate from the attorney's personal and business accounts to protect client interests. Option B reflects the correct ethical duty.

Question 144

Attorney Victor receives a retainer from a client for legal services to be provided in the future. According to the Model Rules of Professional Conduct, what should Victor do with the retainer?

A) Victor may use the retainer for any personal expenses.
B) Victor should deposit the retainer into a trust account and withdraw it as fees are earned.
C) Victor is not required to keep the retainer in a separate account.
D) Victor may use the retainer for any business expenses related to the law firm.

Answer 144: B

Explanation: Under the Model Rules, Attorney Victor should deposit the retainer into a trust account and withdraw it as fees are earned to protect the client's interests. Option B reflects the appropriate ethical duty.

Question 145

Attorney Emma is representing a client in a criminal case. The client insists on testifying falsely during the trial. What should Emma do under the Model Rules of Professional Conduct?

A) Emma must advise the client to testify truthfully, but if the client insists on testifying falsely, Emma may assist in presenting the false testimony.
B) Emma should not take any action, as it is the client's decision whether to testify falsely.
C) Emma may assist the client in testifying falsely as long as it is relevant to the case.
D) Emma must advise the client not to testify falsely and, if necessary, seek permission to withdraw from the representation.

Answer 145: D

Explanation: According to the Model Rules, Attorney Emma's ethical duty is to advise the client not to testify falsely and, if necessary, seek permission to withdraw from the representation. Option D reflects the appropriate ethical response.

Question 146
Under the Model Rules of Professional Conduct, what is the attorney's duty regarding conflicts of interest involving current clients?

A) The attorney should disclose the conflict to the client and continue representing both clients.
B) The attorney is required to withdraw from the representation of both clients.
C) The attorney may continue representing both clients as long as they are in separate matters.
D) The attorney should seek the informed consent of both clients in writing before proceeding.

Answer 146: B
Explanation: Under the Model Rules, when a conflict of interest arises involving current clients, the attorney is required to withdraw from the representation of both clients. Option B reflects the appropriate ethical response.

Question 147
Attorney Rachel receives a settlement offer from opposing counsel but fails to promptly communicate it to her client. Under the Model Rules of Professional Conduct, what is Rachel's ethical duty?

A) Rachel must immediately withdraw from the representation due to her failure to communicate the offer.
B) Rachel should continue representing her client without disclosing the offer.
C) Rachel must promptly communicate the settlement offer to her client.
D) Rachel may communicate the offer to her client only if it is favorable.

Answer 147: C
Explanation: According to the Model Rules, Attorney Rachel's ethical duty is to promptly communicate the settlement offer to her client. Option C reflects the appropriate ethical duty.

Question 148

Under the Model Rules of Professional Conduct, which of the following best describes the duty of an attorney when it comes to the handling of client funds?

A) The attorney may commingle client funds with their personal funds if it is more convenient.
B) The attorney should deposit client funds into a trust account separate from the attorney's personal and business accounts.
C) The attorney is not responsible for keeping records of client funds received.
D) The attorney may use client funds for personal expenses as long as they intend to replenish them later.

Answer 148: B

Explanation: The Model Rules require attorneys to deposit client funds into a trust account separate from the attorney's personal and business accounts to protect client interests. Option B reflects the correct ethical duty.

Question 149

Attorney Victor receives a retainer from a client for legal services to be provided in the future. According to the Model Rules of Professional Conduct, what should Victor do with the retainer?

A) Victor may use the retainer for any personal expenses.
B) Victor should deposit the retainer into a trust account and withdraw it as fees are earned.
C) Victor is not required to keep the retainer in a separate account.
D) Victor may use the retainer for any business expenses related to the law firm.

Answer 149: B

Explanation: Under the Model Rules, Attorney Victor should deposit the retainer into a trust account and withdraw it as fees are earned to protect the client's interests. Option B reflects the appropriate ethical duty.

Question 150
Attorney Emma is representing a client in a criminal case. The client insists on testifying falsely during the trial. What should Emma do under the Model Rules of Professional Conduct?

A) Emma must advise the client to testify truthfully, but if the client insists on testifying falsely, Emma may assist in presenting the false testimony.
B) Emma should not take any action, as it is the client's decision whether to testify falsely.
C) Emma may assist the client in testifying falsely as long as it is relevant to the case.
D) Emma must advise the client not to testify falsely and, if necessary, seek permission to withdraw from the representation.

Answer 150: D
Explanation: According to the Model Rules, Attorney Emma's ethical duty is to advise the client not to testify falsely and, if necessary, seek permission to withdraw from the representation. Option D reflects the appropriate ethical response.

Question 151
Under the Model Rules of Professional Conduct, what is the attorney's duty regarding conflicts of interest involving current clients?

A) The attorney should disclose the conflict to the client and continue representing both clients.
B) The attorney is required to withdraw from the representation of both clients.
C) The attorney may continue representing both clients as long as they are in separate matters.
D) The attorney should seek the informed consent of both clients in writing before proceeding.

Answer 151: B
Explanation: Under the Model Rules, when a conflict of interest arises involving current clients, the attorney is required to withdraw from the representation of both clients. Option B reflects the appropriate ethical response.

Question 152

Attorney Lisa receives a settlement offer from opposing counsel but fails to promptly communicate it to her client. Under the Model Rules of Professional Conduct, what is Lisa's ethical duty?

A) Lisa must immediately withdraw from the representation due to her failure to communicate the offer.
B) Lisa should continue representing her client without disclosing the offer.
C) Lisa must promptly communicate the settlement offer to her client.
D) Lisa may communicate the offer to her client only if it is favorable.

Answer 152: C

Explanation: According to the Model Rules, Attorney Lisa's ethical duty is to promptly communicate the settlement offer to her client. Option C reflects the appropriate ethical duty.

Question 153

Under the Model Rules of Professional Conduct, which of the following best describes the duty of an attorney when it comes to the handling of client funds?

A) The attorney may commingle client funds with their personal funds if it is more convenient.
B) The attorney should deposit client funds into a trust account separate from the attorney's personal and business accounts.
C) The attorney is not responsible for keeping records of client funds received.
D) The attorney may use client funds for personal expenses as long as they intend to replenish them later.

Answer 153: B

Explanation: The Model Rules require attorneys to deposit client funds into a trust account separate from the attorney's personal and business accounts to protect client interests. Option B reflects the correct ethical duty.

Question 154

Attorney Victor receives a retainer from a client for legal services to be provided in the future. According to the Model Rules of Professional Conduct, what should Victor do with the retainer?

A) Victor may use the retainer for any personal expenses.

B) Victor should deposit the retainer into a trust account and withdraw it as fees are earned.
C) Victor is not required to keep the retainer in a separate account.
D) Victor may use the retainer for any business expenses related to the law firm.

Answer 154: B
Explanation: Under the Model Rules, Attorney Victor should deposit the retainer into a trust account and withdraw it as fees are earned to protect the client's interests. Option B reflects the appropriate ethical duty.

Question 155
Attorney Emma is representing a client in a criminal case. The client insists on testifying falsely during the trial. What should Emma do under the Model Rules of Professional Conduct?

A) Emma must advise the client to testify truthfully, but if the client insists on testifying falsely, Emma may assist in presenting the false testimony.
B) Emma should not take any action, as it is the client's decision whether to testify falsely.
C) Emma may assist the client in testifying falsely as long as it is relevant to the case.
D) Emma must advise the client not to testify falsely and, if necessary, seek permission to withdraw from the representation.

Answer 155: D
Explanation: According to the Model Rules, Attorney Emma's ethical duty is to advise the client not to testify falsely and, if necessary, seek permission to withdraw from the representation. Option D reflects the appropriate ethical response.

Question 156
Under the Model Rules of Professional Conduct, what is the attorney's duty regarding conflicts of interest involving current clients?

A) The attorney should disclose the conflict to the client and continue representing both clients.
B) The attorney is required to withdraw from the representation of both clients.
C) The attorney may continue representing both clients as long as they are in separate matters.

D) The attorney should seek the informed consent of both clients in writing before proceeding.

Answer 156: B
Explanation: Under the Model Rules, when a conflict of interest arises involving current clients, the attorney is required to withdraw from the representation of both clients. Option B reflects the appropriate ethical response.

Question 157

Attorney Rachel receives a settlement offer from opposing counsel but fails to promptly communicate it to her client. Under the Model Rules of Professional Conduct, what is Rachel's ethical duty?

A) Rachel must immediately withdraw from the representation due to her failure to communicate the offer.
B) Rachel should continue representing her client without disclosing the offer.
C) Rachel must promptly communicate the settlement offer to her client.
D) Rachel may communicate the offer to her client only if it is favorable.

Answer 157: C
Explanation: According to the Model Rules, Attorney Rachel's ethical duty is to promptly communicate the settlement offer to her client. Option C reflects the appropriate ethical duty.

Question 158

Under the Model Rules of Professional Conduct, which of the following best describes the duty of an attorney when it comes to the handling of client funds?

A) The attorney may commingle client funds with their personal funds if it is more convenient.
B) The attorney should deposit client funds into a trust account separate from the attorney's personal and business accounts.
C) The attorney is not responsible for keeping records of client funds received.
D) The attorney may use client funds for personal expenses as long as they intend to replenish them later.

Answer 158: B

Explanation: The Model Rules require attorneys to deposit client funds into a trust account separate from the attorney's personal and business accounts to protect client interests. Option B reflects the correct ethical duty.

Question 159

Attorney Victor receives a retainer from a client for legal services to be provided in the future. According to the Model Rules of Professional Conduct, what should Victor do with the retainer?

A) Victor may use the retainer for any personal expenses.
B) Victor should deposit the retainer into a trust account and withdraw it as fees are earned.
C) Victor is not required to keep the retainer in a separate account.
D) Victor may use the retainer for any business expenses related to the law firm.

Answer 159: B
Explanation: Under the Model Rules, Attorney Victor should deposit the retainer into a trust account and withdraw it as fees are earned to protect the client's interests. Option B reflects the appropriate ethical duty.

Question 160

Attorney Emma is representing a client in a criminal case. The client insists on testifying falsely during the trial. What should Emma do under the Model Rules of Professional Conduct?

A) Emma must advise the client to testify truthfully, but if the client insists on testifying falsely, Emma may assist in presenting the false testimony.
B) Emma should not take any action, as it is the client's decision whether to testify falsely.
C) Emma may assist the client in testifying falsely as long as it is relevant to the case.
D) Emma must advise the client not to testify falsely and, if necessary, seek permission to withdraw from the representation.

Answer 160: D
Explanation: According to the Model Rules, Attorney Emma's ethical duty is to advise the client not to testify falsely and, if necessary, seek permission to withdraw from the representation. Option D reflects the appropriate ethical response.

Question 161

Under the Model Rules of Professional Conduct, what is the attorney's duty regarding conflicts of interest involving current clients?

A) The attorney should disclose the conflict to the client and continue representing both clients.
B) The attorney is required to withdraw from the representation of both clients.
C) The attorney may continue representing both clients as long as they are in separate matters.
D) The attorney should seek the informed consent of both clients in writing before proceeding.

Answer 161: B
Explanation: Under the Model Rules, when a conflict of interest arises involving current clients, the attorney is required to withdraw from the representation of both clients. Option B reflects the appropriate ethical response.

Question 162

Attorney Lisa receives a settlement offer from opposing counsel but fails to promptly communicate it to her client. Under the Model Rules of Professional Conduct, what is Lisa's ethical duty?

A) Lisa must immediately withdraw from the representation due to her failure to communicate the offer.
B) Lisa should continue representing her client without disclosing the offer.
C) Lisa must promptly communicate the settlement offer to her client.
D) Lisa may communicate the offer to her client only if it is favorable.

Answer 162: C
Explanation: According to the Model Rules, Attorney Lisa's ethical duty is to promptly communicate the settlement offer to her client. Option C reflects the appropriate ethical duty.

Question 163
Under the Model Rules of Professional Conduct, which of the following best describes the duty of an attorney when it comes to the handling of client funds?

A) The attorney may commingle client funds with their personal funds if it is more convenient.
B) The attorney should deposit client funds into a trust account separate from the attorney's personal and business accounts.
C) The attorney is not responsible for keeping records of client funds received.
D) The attorney may use client funds for personal expenses as long as they intend to replenish them later.

Answer 163: B
Explanation: The Model Rules require attorneys to deposit client funds into a trust account separate from the attorney's personal and business accounts to protect client interests. Option B reflects the correct ethical duty.

Question 164
Attorney Victor receives a retainer from a client for legal services to be provided in the future. According to the Model Rules of Professional Conduct, what should Victor do with the retainer?

A) Victor may use the retainer for any personal expenses.
B) Victor should deposit the retainer into a trust account and withdraw it as fees are earned.
C) Victor is not required to keep the retainer in a separate account.
D) Victor may use the retainer for any business expenses related to the law firm.

Answer 164: B
Explanation: Under the Model Rules, Attorney Victor should deposit the retainer into a trust account and withdraw it as fees are earned to protect the client's interests. Option B reflects the appropriate ethical duty.

Question 165
Attorney Emma is representing a client in a criminal case. The client insists on testifying falsely during the trial. What should Emma do under the Model Rules of Professional Conduct?

A) Emma must advise the client to testify truthfully, but if the client insists on testifying falsely, Emma may assist in presenting the false testimony.
B) Emma should not take any action, as it is the client's decision whether to testify falsely.
C) Emma may assist the client in testifying falsely as long as it is relevant to the case.
D) Emma must advise the client not to testify falsely and, if necessary, seek permission to withdraw from the representation.

Answer 165: D
Explanation: According to the Model Rules, Attorney Emma's ethical duty is to advise the client not to testify falsely and, if necessary, seek permission to withdraw from the representation. Option D reflects the appropriate ethical response.

Question 166
Under the Model Rules of Professional Conduct, what is the attorney's duty regarding conflicts of interest involving current clients?

A) The attorney should disclose the conflict to the client and continue representing both clients.
B) The attorney is required to withdraw from the representation of both clients.
C) The attorney may continue representing both clients as long as they are in separate matters.
D) The attorney should seek the informed consent of both clients in writing before proceeding.

Answer 166: B
Explanation: Under the Model Rules, when a conflict of interest arises involving current clients, the attorney is required to withdraw from the representation of both clients. Option B reflects the appropriate ethical response.

Question 167
Attorney Rachel receives a settlement offer from opposing counsel but fails to promptly communicate it to her client. Under the Model Rules of Professional Conduct, what is Rachel's ethical duty?

A) Rachel must immediately withdraw from the representation due to her failure to communicate the offer.

B) Rachel should continue representing her client without disclosing the offer.
C) Rachel must promptly communicate the settlement offer to her client.
D) Rachel may communicate the offer to her client only if it is favorable.

Answer 167: C
Explanation: According to the Model Rules, Attorney Rachel's ethical duty is to promptly communicate the settlement offer to her client. Option C reflects the appropriate ethical duty.

Question 168
Under the Model Rules of Professional Conduct, which of the following best describes the duty of an attorney when it comes to the handling of client funds?

A) The attorney may commingle client funds with their personal funds if it is more convenient.
B) The attorney should deposit client funds into a trust account separate from the attorney's personal and business accounts.
C) The attorney is not responsible for keeping records of client funds received.
D) The attorney may use client funds for personal expenses as long as they intend to replenish them later.

Answer 168: B
Explanation: The Model Rules require attorneys to deposit client funds into a trust account separate from the attorney's personal and business accounts to protect client interests. Option B reflects the correct ethical duty.

Question 169
Attorney Victor receives a retainer from a client for legal services to be provided in the future. According to the Model Rules of Professional Conduct, what should Victor do with the retainer?

A) Victor may use the retainer for any personal expenses.
B) Victor should deposit the retainer into a trust account and withdraw it as fees are earned.
C) Victor is not required to keep the retainer in a separate account.
D) Victor may use the retainer for any business expenses related to the law firm.

Answer 169: B

Explanation: Under the Model Rules, Attorney Victor should deposit the retainer into a trust account and withdraw it as fees are earned to protect the client's interests. Option B reflects the appropriate ethical duty.

Question 170

Attorney Emma is representing a client in a criminal case. The client insists on testifying falsely during the trial. What should Emma do under the Model Rules of Professional Conduct?

A) Emma must advise the client to testify truthfully, but if the client insists on testifying falsely, Emma may assist in presenting the false testimony.
B) Emma should not take any action, as it is the client's decision whether to testify falsely.
C) Emma may assist the client in testifying falsely as long as it is relevant to the case.
D) Emma must advise the client not to testify falsely and, if necessary, seek permission to withdraw from the representation.

Answer 170: D
Explanation: According to the Model Rules, Attorney Emma's ethical duty is to advise the client not to testify falsely and, if necessary, seek permission to withdraw from the representation. Option D reflects the appropriate ethical response.

Question 171

Under the Model Rules of Professional Conduct, what is the attorney's duty regarding conflicts of interest involving current clients?

A) The attorney should disclose the conflict to the client and continue representing both clients.
B) The attorney is required to withdraw from the representation of both clients.
C) The attorney may continue representing both clients as long as they are in separate matters.
D) The attorney should seek the informed consent of both clients in writing before proceeding.

Answer 171: B
Explanation: Under the Model Rules, when a conflict of interest arises involving current clients, the attorney is required to withdraw from the

representation of both clients. Option B reflects the appropriate ethical response.

Question 172
Attorney Lisa receives a settlement offer from opposing counsel but fails to promptly communicate it to her client. Under the Model Rules of Professional Conduct, what is Lisa's ethical duty?

A) Lisa must immediately withdraw from the representation due to her failure to communicate the offer.
B) Lisa should continue representing her client without disclosing the offer.
C) Lisa must promptly communicate the settlement offer to her client.
D) Lisa may communicate the offer to her client only if it is favorable.

Answer 172: C
Explanation: According to the Model Rules, Attorney Lisa's ethical duty is to promptly communicate the settlement offer to her client. Option C reflects the appropriate ethical duty.

Question 173
Under the Model Rules of Professional Conduct, which of the following best describes the duty of an attorney when it comes to the handling of client funds?

A) The attorney may commingle client funds with their personal funds if it is more convenient.
B) The attorney should deposit client funds into a trust account separate from the attorney's personal and business accounts.
C) The attorney is not responsible for keeping records of client funds received.
D) The attorney may use client funds for personal expenses as long as they intend to replenish them later.

Answer 173: B
Explanation: The Model Rules require attorneys to deposit client funds into a trust account separate from the attorney's personal and business accounts to protect client interests. Option B reflects the correct ethical duty.

Question 174

Attorney Victor receives a retainer from a client for legal services to be provided in the future. According to the Model Rules of Professional Conduct, what should Victor do with the retainer?

A) Victor may use the retainer for any personal expenses.
B) Victor should deposit the retainer into a trust account and withdraw it as fees are earned.
C) Victor is not required to keep the retainer in a separate account.
D) Victor may use the retainer for any business expenses related to the law firm.

Answer 174: B

Explanation: Under the Model Rules, Attorney Victor should deposit the retainer into a trust account and withdraw it as fees are earned to protect the client's interests. Option B reflects the appropriate ethical duty.

Question 175

Attorney Emma is representing a client in a criminal case. The client insists on testifying falsely during the trial. What should Emma do under the Model Rules of Professional Conduct?

A) Emma must advise the client to testify truthfully, but if the client insists on testifying falsely, Emma may assist in presenting the false testimony.
B) Emma should not take any action, as it is the client's decision whether to testify falsely.
C) Emma may assist the client in testifying falsely as long as it is relevant to the case.
D) Emma must advise the client not to testify falsely and, if necessary, seek permission to withdraw from the representation.

Answer 175: D

Explanation: According to the Model Rules, Attorney Emma's ethical duty is to advise the client not to testify falsely and, if necessary, seek permission to withdraw from the representation. Option D reflects the appropriate ethical response.

Question 176

Under the Model Rules of Professional Conduct, what is the attorney's duty regarding conflicts of interest involving current clients?

A) The attorney should disclose the conflict to the client and continue representing both clients.
B) The attorney is required to withdraw from the representation of both clients.
C) The attorney may continue representing both clients as long as they are in separate matters.
D) The attorney should seek the informed consent of both clients in writing before proceeding.

Answer 176: B
Explanation: Under the Model Rules, when a conflict of interest arises involving current clients, the attorney is required to withdraw from the representation of both clients. Option B reflects the appropriate ethical response.

Question 177

Attorney Lisa receives a settlement offer from opposing counsel but fails to promptly communicate it to her client. Under the Model Rules of Professional Conduct, what is Lisa's ethical duty?

A) Lisa must immediately withdraw from the representation due to her failure to communicate the offer.
B) Lisa should continue representing her client without disclosing the offer.
C) Lisa must promptly communicate the settlement offer to her client.
D) Lisa may communicate the offer to her client only if it is favorable.

Answer 177: C
Explanation: According to the Model Rules, Attorney Lisa's ethical duty is to promptly communicate the settlement offer to her client. Option C reflects the appropriate ethical duty.

Question 178

Under the Model Rules of Professional Conduct, which of the following best describes the duty of an attorney when it comes to the handling of client funds?

A) The attorney may commingle client funds with their personal funds if it is more convenient.
B) The attorney should deposit client funds into a trust account separate from the attorney's personal and business accounts.
C) The attorney is not responsible for keeping records of client funds received.
D) The attorney may use client funds for personal expenses as long as they intend to replenish them later.

Answer 178: B

Explanation: The Model Rules require attorneys to deposit client funds into a trust account separate from the attorney's personal and business accounts to protect client interests. Option B reflects the correct ethical duty.

Question 179

Attorney Victor receives a retainer from a client for legal services to be provided in the future. According to the Model Rules of Professional Conduct, what should Victor do with the retainer?

A) Victor may use the retainer for any personal expenses.
B) Victor should deposit the retainer into a trust account and withdraw it as fees are earned.
C) Victor is not required to keep the retainer in a separate account.
D) Victor may use the retainer for any business expenses related to the law firm.

Answer 179: B

Explanation: Under the Model Rules, Attorney Victor should deposit the retainer into a trust account and withdraw it as fees are earned to protect the client's interests. Option B reflects the appropriate ethical duty.

Question 180

Attorney Emma is representing a client in a criminal case. The client insists on testifying falsely during the trial. What should Emma do under the Model Rules of Professional Conduct?

A) Emma must advise the client to testify truthfully, but if the client insists on testifying falsely, Emma may assist in presenting the false testimony.
B) Emma should not take any action, as it is the client's decision whether to testify falsely.
C) Emma may assist the client in testifying falsely as long as it is relevant to the case.
D) Emma must advise the client not to testify falsely and, if necessary, seek permission to withdraw from the representation.

Answer 180: D
Explanation: According to the Model Rules, Attorney Emma's ethical duty is to advise the client not to testify falsely and, if necessary, seek permission to withdraw from the representation. Option D reflects the appropriate ethical response.

Question 181

In a disciplinary matter involving an attorney, the burden of proof is typically on:

A) The attorney to prove their innocence.
B) The client who initiated the complaint.
C) The disciplinary authority bringing the charges.
D) The judge overseeing the matter.

Answer 181: C
Explanation: In disciplinary matters involving attorneys, the burden of proof typically rests on the disciplinary authority bringing the charges. Option C is the correct choice.

Question 182

Which of the following best defines "imputed conflicts of interest" as described in the Model Rules of Professional Conduct?

A) Conflicts of interest that an attorney intentionally creates for their own benefit.
B) Conflicts of interest that arise when an attorney has a personal interest that could affect their professional judgment.
C) Conflicts of interest that occur between two clients represented by the same law firm.
D) Conflicts of interest that are impossible to resolve in an attorney's practice.

Answer 182: C

Explanation: "Imputed conflicts of interest" as described in the Model Rules refer to conflicts of interest that occur between two clients represented by the same law firm. Option C is the correct definition.

Question 183

What is the primary purpose of the attorney-client privilege in the legal profession?

A) To allow attorneys to refuse to answer questions in court.
B) To protect clients' confidential communications with their attorneys.
C) To shield attorneys from disciplinary actions.
D) To encourage attorneys to share information with their colleagues.

Answer 183: B

Explanation: The primary purpose of the attorney-client privilege is to protect clients' confidential communications with their attorneys, allowing clients to speak freely and honestly with their attorneys. Option B is the correct purpose.

Question 184

Which of the following statements best describes a conflict of interest that is not waivable under the Model Rules of Professional Conduct?

A) A conflict that may be resolved through full disclosure and the informed consent of the affected clients.
B) A conflict that could compromise an attorney's professional judgment.
C) A conflict that arises between a client and the attorney's personal interests.
D) A conflict that is unmitigated and creates a significant risk to the representation.

Answer 184: D
Explanation: A conflict of interest that is not waivable under the Model Rules of Professional Conduct is one that is unmitigated and creates a significant risk to the representation. Option D correctly describes such conflicts.

Question 185

Under the Model Rules of Professional Conduct, when can an attorney reveal client confidences without the client's informed consent?

A) When the attorney believes it is in the client's best interest to do so.
B) Only with a court order or to prevent death or substantial bodily harm.
C) Whenever the attorney deems it necessary to protect their own interests.
D) Whenever the attorney believes it is necessary to advance their own career.

Answer 185: B
Explanation: An attorney can reveal client confidences without the client's informed consent only with a court order or to prevent death or substantial bodily harm under the Model Rules of Professional Conduct. Option B is the correct choice.

Question 186

Which Model Rule of Professional Conduct pertains to the duty of an attorney to maintain client confidences and protect the attorney-client privilege?

A) Model Rule 1.1 (Competence)
B) Model Rule 1.2 (Scope of Representation)
C) Model Rule 1.6 (Confidentiality of Information)
D) Model Rule 1.9 (Duties to Former Clients)

Answer 186: C

Explanation: The duty of an attorney to maintain client confidences and protect the attorney-client privilege is addressed in Model Rule 1.6 (Confidentiality of Information). Option C is the correct rule.

Question 187

What is the term used to describe the principle that attorneys must act in the best interests of their clients and diligently represent their clients' lawful objectives?

A) The duty of loyalty.
B) The duty of competence.
C) The duty of honesty.
D) The duty of confidentiality.

Answer 187: A

Explanation: The principle that attorneys must act in the best interests of their clients and diligently represent their clients' lawful objectives is known as the duty of loyalty. Option A is the correct term.

Question 188

What does the attorney-client privilege protect?

A) Any communication between an attorney and a client, even if it involves illegal activities.
B) All written and electronic records in an attorney's office.
C) Communications made in furtherance of the client's intent to commit a crime.
D) Confidential communications between an attorney and a client for the purpose of legal advice.

Answer 188: D

Explanation: The attorney-client privilege protects confidential communications between an attorney and a client for the purpose of legal advice. Option D accurately describes the protection.

Question 189
Under the Model Rules of Professional Conduct, what is the primary duty of an attorney when representing a client?

A) To minimize the attorney's fees and expenses.
B) To provide pro bono services to the client.
C) To diligently and zealously represent the client's lawful interests.
D) To make all case decisions unilaterally without consulting the client.

Answer 189: C
Explanation: The primary duty of an attorney when representing a client, as per the Model Rules of Professional Conduct, is to diligently and zealously represent the client's lawful interests. Option C reflects the correct duty.

Question 190
What is the term used to describe the legal concept that allows an attorney to withdraw from representation if the client's objectives are repugnant or the client insists on taking actions that violate the law?

A) The attorney-client privilege.
B) The doctrine of informed consent.
C) The right to disclosure.
D) The permissive withdrawal.

Answer 190: D
Explanation: The legal concept that allows an attorney to withdraw from representation if the client's objectives are repugnant or the client insists on taking actions that violate the law is known as "permissive withdrawal." Option D is the correct term.

Question 191
Under the Model Rules of Professional Conduct, when can an attorney reveal client confidences to prevent the client from committing a crime or fraud that is reasonably certain to result in substantial injury to the financial interests of another?

A) Only with the client's informed consent.
B) Never, as client confidences are always protected.
C) When the attorney believes it is in the client's best interest.
D) When the attorney's disclosure is necessary to prevent the crime or fraud.

Answer 191: D

Explanation: Under the Model Rules of Professional Conduct, an attorney can reveal client confidences to prevent the client from committing a crime or fraud that is reasonably certain to result in substantial injury to the financial interests of another, provided that the attorney's disclosure is necessary. Option D is the correct condition.

Question 192

Which of the following is considered a conflict of interest under the Model Rules of Professional Conduct?

A) A conflict that arises when an attorney must choose between representing a client and testifying as a witness in the same matter.
B) A conflict that occurs when an attorney shares office space with another attorney from a different law firm.
C) A conflict that arises when an attorney represents two clients who are siblings in unrelated matters.
D) A conflict that occurs when an attorney has a personal interest that may affect their professional judgment.

Answer 192: A

Explanation: A conflict that arises when an attorney must choose between representing a client and testifying as a witness in the same matter is considered a conflict of interest under the Model Rules of Professional Conduct. Option A accurately describes such a conflict.

Question 193

What is the primary purpose of the attorney-client privilege in the legal profession?

A) To allow attorneys to refuse to answer questions in court.
B) To protect clients' confidential communications with their attorneys.
C) To shield attorneys from disciplinary actions.
D) To encourage attorneys to share information with their colleagues.

Answer 193: B

Explanation: The primary purpose of the attorney-client privilege is to protect clients' confidential communications with their attorneys, allowing clients to speak freely and honestly with their attorneys. Option B is the correct purpose.

Question 194
Under the Model Rules of Professional Conduct, what is the attorney's duty when it comes to fees and expenses in a representation?

A) The attorney must charge the highest possible fees to maximize their income.
B) The attorney may refuse representation if the client cannot pay the fees.
C) The attorney should communicate the basis for their fees and expenses to the client.
D) The attorney is not required to keep records of fees and expenses.

Answer 194: C
Explanation: Under the Model Rules of Professional Conduct, the attorney's duty regarding fees and expenses includes communicating the basis for their fees and expenses to the client. Option C reflects the appropriate duty.

Question 195
What is the term used to describe the ethical duty of an attorney to keep the client's information and confidences private?

A) The attorney-client privilege.
B) The duty of loyalty.
C) The duty of competence.
D) The duty of confidentiality.

Answer 195: D
Explanation: The ethical duty of an attorney to keep the client's information and confidences private is known as the duty of confidentiality. Option D is the correct term.

Question 196
Under the Model Rules of Professional Conduct, what is the attorney's responsibility if they become aware of a conflict of interest between two clients?

A) The attorney should inform one client about the conflict and proceed with representation.
B) The attorney should withdraw from the representation of one or both clients.

C) The attorney may continue to represent both clients as long as they obtain written informed consent.

D) The attorney is not required to take any action regarding the conflict.

Answer 196: B

Explanation: Under the Model Rules of Professional Conduct, the attorney's responsibility when they become aware of a conflict of interest between two clients is to withdraw from the representation of one or both clients. Option B reflects the correct ethical response.

Question 197

What does the doctrine of informed consent require in the context of conflicts of interest?

A) Clients must be informed about the attorney's personal conflicts of interest.

B) Clients must give their consent for all actions taken by the attorney.

C) Clients must be informed about potential conflicts of interest and provide their consent in writing.

D) Clients must be informed about all legal issues related to their case.

Answer 197: C

Explanation: In the context of conflicts of interest, the doctrine of informed consent requires that clients be informed about potential conflicts of interest and provide their consent in writing. Option C is the correct requirement.

Question 198

Under the Model Rules of Professional Conduct, what is the attorney's duty regarding communication with the client?

A) The attorney may communicate with the client only when it is convenient for the attorney.

B) The attorney should keep the client informed about the status of the matter and promptly respond to the client's reasonable requests for information.

C) The attorney is not required to communicate with the client once representation has commenced.

D) The attorney must communicate with the client only in writing.

Answer 198: B

Explanation: Under the Model Rules of Professional Conduct, the attorney's duty regarding communication with the client includes keeping the client informed about the status of the matter and promptly responding to the client's reasonable requests for information. Option B reflects the appropriate duty.

Question 199
What is the term used to describe a situation where an attorney withdraws from a representation due to the client's illegal or fraudulent actions?

A) Permissive withdrawal.
B) Mandatory withdrawal.
C) Conflict of interest.
D) Withdrawal with informed consent.

Answer 199: B
Explanation: A situation where an attorney withdraws from a representation due to the client's illegal or fraudulent actions is referred to as "mandatory withdrawal." Option B is the correct term.

Question 200
In the context of conflicts of interest, what is meant by "informed consent" under the Model Rules of Professional Conduct?

A) The client's agreement to pay the attorney's fees.
B) The client's understanding of the attorney's personal interests.
C) The client's agreement to the attorney's decisions without question.
D) The client's agreement to the conflict after being provided with full disclosure and understanding of the relevant facts.

Answer 200: D
Explanation: In the context of conflicts of interest, "informed consent" under the Model Rules of Professional Conduct refers to the client's agreement to the conflict after being provided with full disclosure and understanding of the relevant facts. Option D accurately describes informed consent.

Made in the USA
Columbia, SC
15 October 2024

44401456R00143